George Cooper

The Origin of Financial Crises

Dr. George Cooper is a principal of Alignment Investors, a division of BlueCrest Capital Management Ltd. He was born in Sunderland and studied at Durham University. George has worked as a fund manager at Goldman Sachs and as strategist for Deutsche Bank and JPMorgan. He lives in London with his wife and two children.

The Origin of Financial Crises

Central banks, credit bubbles and the efficient market fallacy

George Cooper

Vintage Books

A Division of Random House, Inc.

New York

FIRST VINTAGE BOOKS EDITION, DECEMBER 2008

Copyright © 2008 by George Cooper

All rights reserved. Published in the United States by Vintage Books,
a division of Random House, Inc., New York.
Originally published in slightly different form
in hardcover in Great Britain by Harriman House in 2008.

Vintage and colophon are registered trademarks of
Random House, Inc.

The Cataloging-in-Publication Data is on file
at the Library of Congress.

Vintage ISBN: 978-0-307-47345-5

www.vintagebooks.com

Printed in the United States of America
10 9 8 7 6 5 4 3

Contents

Acknowledgements

During my years as a fixed income analyst I have been lucky enough to have had the opportunity to discuss, debate, and, not infrequently, argue about financial market instability and central bank policy with some of the financial markets' finest analysts. I owe a broad debt of gratitude both to former colleagues, clients and a few senior central bankers for having helped develop and refine some of the ideas discussed here.

For helpful suggestions on the draft manuscript I owe thanks to Philip Maidens, Richard Williams, Dr Wendy Hamilton and Stephane Monier. I am also eternally grateful to my wife and family for their patience during the writing process.

Preface to the Vintage Edition

In the six months since I completed this book the financial crisis has intensified to the point at which, in October 2008, the entire global banking system came close to collapse. If it were not for the announcement of massive state-funded bailout packages, it is probable that not just the financial markets but also our global trade system would have ceased to operate. In this globally interdependent world, the consequences of such a failure are unimaginable.

Hopefully history will record the failure of Lehman Brothers and the weeks leading up to the October's bailouts as the most intense phase of the financial crisis; but even if this proves to be the case, the consequences of these events for the broader economy are only just becoming apparent. Capital losses, shattered confidence and the drag of a partially nationalised banking system will impair economic progress for years to come.

Our leaders have now set about the inevitable process of apportioning blame and tightening regulatory control. Better regulation is certainly needed and in places tighter regulation is needed. That said, history suggests that regulation designed for the last crisis does not prevent the next; tighter accounting standards after the dot-com bubble did nothing to prevent the subsequent housing bubble. To prevent the next crisis, we must look beyond the details of today's mortgage bubble to the underlying monetary system which helped facilitate it. Current events represent the wholesale failure of monetary policy as practiced over recent decades. Improving bank regulation is important; reforming central bank monetary policy is essential, and these reforms are required at both the national and international level.

George Cooper

October 2008

Preface to the Original Edition

This book has been written, in response to the current credit crisis, to explain why the global economy, and the U.S. economy in particular, finds itself caught in a seemingly endless procession of asset price bubbles, followed by devastating credit crunches. It describes the processes that generate these cycles and the reasons behind the policy mistakes that have, of late, tended to exacerbate them.

My aim is to bring an understanding of financial instability and central banking to as wide an audience as possible in the hope that this will bring with it an informed discussion of how macroeconomic policy should be reformed. If we are to break out of this damaging cycle of booms and busts, all participants in the economy must recognise the proper role and limitations of macroeconomic policy. Politicians and voters must acknowledge that it is neither possible nor desirable to use fiscal and monetary policy to immediately counteract any and all economic downturns. Central banks must return to their core purpose of managing the credit creation process and must learn to resist political and private sector pressure for an endless credit-fuelled economic expansion.

The central thesis of this book is that our financial system does not behave according to the laws of the Efficient Market Hypothesis, as laid down by the conventional wisdom of today's prevailing economic theory. The Efficient Market Hypothesis describes our financial system as a docile animal that, left to its own devices, will settle into a steady optimal equilibrium. By contrast, this book argues our financial system is inherently unstable, has no steady state equilibrium and is habitually prone to the formation of damaging boom-bust cycles. It is argued that this instability requires central banks to manage the credit creation process. However, it is also explained how central bank policy can inadvertently slip from providing a stabilising influence on economic activity to one that, over time, amplifies boom-bust cycles and destabilises our economies.

It will be argued that the U.S. Federal Reserve has inadvertently slipped into a mode of monetary policy that is generating a series of ever-larger credit cycles and which, if continued, will significantly impair the prospects of what is still the world's most important and most vibrant economy.

George Cooper

April 2008

1

Introduction

1.1 Lopsided Policy

The first years of this millennium were marred with a corporate credit crisis; this being the hangover of a credit binge associated with the stock market boom of the late 1990s. Just as this crisis ebbed we found ourselves engulfed in a housing boom and, sure as night follows day, this boom has now morphed into its inevitable credit crunch. The proximity of these boom-bust cycles has fuelled the popular perception that financial crises are becoming larger and more frequent. The following chapters will explain why this popular perception is correct.

Toward the end of the book I make some policy suggestions that, it is hoped, could begin to dampen the current chain of overlapping boom-bust cycles. The overall thrust of these suggestions is that avoiding the financial tsunamis comes at the price of permitting, even encouraging, a greater number of smaller credit cycles. And also at the price of requiring central banks to occasionally halt credit expansions. That is to say, the central banks must be required to prick asset price bubbles. Key to the success of any such policy will be a political climate that accepts the need for symmetric monetary policy; excessive credit expansion should be fought with the same vigour as is used to fight excessive credit contraction. As things stand neither politicians nor voters are ready for such tough love and central bankers have neither the stomach nor inclination to deliver it. In large part this is because economists have taught us that it is unwise and unnecessary to combat asset price bubbles and excessive credit creation. Even if we were unwise enough to wish to prick an asset price bubble, we are told it is impossible to see the bubble while it is in its inflationary phase. We are told, however, that by some unspecified means the bubble's camouflage is lifted immediately as it begins deflating, thereby providing a trigger for prompt fiscal and monetary stimulus.

In recent years this lopsided approach to monetary and fiscal policy has been further refined into what has been described as a "risk management paradigm", whereby policy makers attempt to get their retaliation in early by easing policy in anticipation of an economic slowdown, even before firm evidence of the slowdown has been accumulated. This strategy is perhaps best described as pre-emptive asymmetric monetary policy.

To followers of orthodox economic theory, based on the presumption of efficient financial markets, this new flavour of monetary policy can be justified. Yet, current events suggest these asymmetric policies have gone badly wrong, leading not to a higher average economic growth rate, as was hoped, but instead to a an unsustainable level of borrowing ending in abrupt credit crunches.

1.2 Efficient Markets – More Faith Than Fact

The bare outlines of a competitive profit-and-loss system are simple to describe. Everything has a price – each commodity and each service. Even the different kinds of human labor have prices, usually called 'wage rates.'

Everybody receives money for what he sells and uses this money to buy what he wishes. If more is wanted of any one good, say shoes, a flood of new orders will be given for it. This will cause its price to rise and more to be produced. Similarly, if more is available of a good like tea than people want, its price will be marked down as a result of competition. At the lower price people will drink more tea, and producers will no longer produce so much. Thus equilibrium of supply and demand will be restored.

What is true of the markets for consumers' goods is also true of markets for factors of production such as labor, land, and capital inputs.

Paul A Samuelson[1]

Who could possibly argue with the above passage? It was written by one of the world's most respected economists and is no more than a statement of the common-sense principle of supply and demand. When the demand for a particular product goes up, so does its price, which is then followed by an increase in supply. According to this theory, prices jostle up and down keeping supply and demand in perfect balance. With just a little more thought we can stretch the argument further and convince ourselves not only that this process generates a stable equilibrium state, but that it also ensures the best possible arrangement of prices, leading to the optimal allocation of resources; if a better, more-economically productive, allocation of resources could be achieved, then those able to make better use of the resources would be able to pay more for them, causing prices to change accordingly. Naturally, if markets tend toward an optimal arrangement of prices, with the most productive allocation of resources, this configuration must also be a stable equilibrium situation. The upshot of all of this is what is known as the laissez-faire[2] school of economic theory, which argues that market forces be given free rein to do as they choose. The logic of the laissez-faire school being that, if free markets naturally achieve an optimal equilibrium, any interference with market forces can at best achieve nothing, but more likely will push the system away from equilibrium toward a sub-optimal state. The prevailing laissez-faire

---

[1] "Economics, An Introductory Analysis" Paul A. Samuelson, p39, fourth edition.

[2] A French phrase meaning 'let do' which has been adopted as a shorthand phrase implying a strategy of allowing markets to operate with complete freedom, unhindered by any form of management, regulation or other government interference.

school therefore requires the minimization, even elimination, of all forms of interference with the operation of market processes.

It also follows from the efficient market philosophy that only external adverse shocks are able to push markets away from their natural optimal state, as, by definition, an equilibrium-seeking system cannot internally generate destabilising forces able to push it away from equilibrium.

1.3 A Slight Of Hand

Now re-read Samuelson's passage, only this time look out for the slight of hand in the final sentence:

> What is true of the markets for consumers' goods is also true of markets for factors of production such as labor, land, and capital inputs.

The passage provides a convincing explanation of how equilibrium is established in the marketplace for goods, but when it comes to the markets for labour, land and capital inputs, there is no explanation of the mechanisms through which equilibrium is established. For these markets we are offered nothing better than proof by assertion. This logical trick is pervasive in economic teaching: we are first persuaded that the markets for goods are efficient, and then beguiled into believing this to be a general principle applicable to all markets. As the failure of Northern Rock and Bear Stearns show it is unsafe to assume that all markets are inherently stable.

1.4 The Market For Bling

We can easily find a counter example to Samuelson's well-behaved supply-and-demand driven markets. In the marketplace for fine art and luxury goods, demand is frequently stimulated precisely because supply cannot be increased in the manner required for market efficiency: Who would pay $140,000,000 for a Jackson Pollock painting if supply could be increased in proportion to demand? The phrase "conspicuous consumption" was coined by the economist Thorstein Veblen to describe markets where demand rose rather than declined with price. Veblen's theory was that in these markets it was the high price, the *publically* high price, of the object that generated the demand for it. Veblen argued that the wealthy used the purchase of high-priced goods to signal their economic status.[3] Veblen was the original economist of bling – if you've got it you want to flaunt it.

Fortunately for the high priests of market efficiency, Veblen's observations can be dismissed as minor distortions within an overall economic environment that responds in a rational manner to higher prices. That is to say, even at a price of $140,000,000, the market for Jackson Pollock paintings is irrelevant to the wider economy.

1.5 When The Absence Of Supply Drives Demand

While the markets for bling can be dismissed as economically irrelevant, there are other much more important markets which also defy the laws of supply and demand, as described by Samuelson. While Veblen identified the rare conditions in which high prices promoted high demand, we can also consider the much more common situation in which low or falling supply promotes high demand.

Today's oil markets are a case in point, where constrained supply is prompting higher speculative demand. While consumers of oil are reducing their oil purchases in response to supply constraints and higher

---

3 "The Theory of the Leisure Class" Thorstein Veblen, first published 1899.

prices, speculators (investors) in oil are moving in the opposite direction and increasing their purchases.

This simple observation of how consumers and speculators respond in different ways to supply constraints gives us the first hint that a fundamentally different market mechanism operates in the markets for assets to that which dominates the markets for goods and services. This effect is not confined just to today's unusual oil market: Who would invest in the shares of a company if that company were in the habit of issuing more stock whenever its share price rose above a certain level?

As a rule, when we invest we are looking for an asset with a degree of scarcity value, one for which supply cannot be increased to meet demand. Whenever we invest in the hope of achieving capital gains we are seeking scarcity value, in defiance of the core principle that supply can move in response to demand.

To the extent that asset price changes can be seen as a signal of an asset becoming more or less scarce, we can see how asset markets may behave in a manner similar to those of Veblen's market for conspicuous consumption goods. In Veblen's case it is simply high prices that generate high demand, but in asset markets it is the rate of change of prices that stimulates shifting demand.

Frequently in asset markets demand does not stimulate supply, rather a lack of supply stimulates demand. Equally price rises can signal a lack of supply thereby generating additional demand, or, conversely, price falls can signal a glut of supply triggering reduced demand.

1.6 Introducing The Efficient Market Hypothesis

To economists the importance of efficient markets lies not in the markets' pricing mechanism directly, but rather in the ability of the pricing mechanism to maximise economic output via an optimal allocation of resources. To financial professionals the emphasis is more directly on the pricing of the items being traded. Financial theory has refined and extended the implications of market efficiency into an additional set of laws describing how markets must behave as a consequence of their being efficient.

The key message of the Efficient Market Hypothesis is that asset prices are *always and everywhere* at the correct price. That is to say, today's market prices, no matter what they are, correctly reflect assets' true values, based on both current economic conditions and the best estimate of how those conditions will evolve in the future. According to this financial theory any asset price movement must be generated by external "shocks". To the efficient market school the constant price changes observed in financial markets are the result of those markets responding to a constant stream of new information.

The Efficient Market Hypothesis has no room for asset price bubbles or busts; under this theory the wild asset price swings commonly referred to as bubbles are nothing more than markets responding to changing fundamentals. People outside of the world of economics and finance may be amazed to know that a significant body of researchers are still engaged in the task of proving that the pricing of the NASDAQ stock market correctly reflected the market's true value throughout the period commonly known as the NASDAQ bubble. To these researchers the NASDAQ Composite Index was correctly priced at 1,140 in March 1996, also correctly priced at 5,048 in March 2000, and again correctly priced when, in October 2002, it had returned to a price of 1,140. The intellectual contortions required to rationalize all of these prices beggars belief, but the contortions are performed, none the less, in the name of defending the Efficient Market Hypothesis.[4]

The idea that markets are always correctly priced remains a key argument against central banks attempting to prick asset price bubbles. Strangely, however, when asset prices begin falling the new lower prices are immediately recognised as being somehow wrong and requiring corrective action on the part of policy makers.

Another interesting result of the Efficient Market Hypothesis is that it can be used to infer the manner in which asset prices move, which in turn allows for the calculation of the entire probability distribution of potential future asset returns. Sadly, these theoretical distributions tend not to fit with the reality of financial markets, which in practice tend to generate extremes of both positive and negative returns that simply cannot be explained with the statistical models derived from the Efficient Market Hypothesis. The clash between the theoretical statistics predicted by efficient markets and those observed within real financial markets is known as the "fat tails" problem.[5] One recent example of the fat tail problem occurred with huge losses in one of the world's largest hedge funds. These losses were apparently described by the firm's chief financial officer as resulting from the fund suffering adverse "25-standard deviation events, several days in a row". It is difficult to convey just how improbable a pair of back-to-back 25-standard

---

[4] See "Was there a Nasdaq bubble in the late 1990s?" L Pastor, Pietro Veronesi, Journal of Financial Economics, Vol 81, Issue 1, July 2006. The paper's answer to the question posed in its title: 'Not necessarily: a firm's fundamental value increases with uncertainty about average future profitability, and this uncertainty was unusually high in the late 1990s' – Apparently we should pay more for companies about which we know less! One suspects this wisdom has yet to reach Warren Buffett.

[5] The term "fat tails" refers to the tendency for distributions of asset returns not to follow bell-shaped "normal" distribution curves, but instead to have an excess of events recorded in wings or tails of the distribution. Frequently asset return distributions look quite unlike normal distributions and can often be double peaked.

deviation losses really is, but by my estimate its probability is roughly:

0.00000000000000000000000000000000000000000000000000000000000
00000000000000000000000000000000000000000000000000000000000000
00000000000000000000000000000000000000000000000000000000000000
00000000000000000000000000000000000000000000000000000000000000
0000000000000000000000000000000000000000000000000000001.

Statistically speaking, a pair of 25-standard deviation events is not an example of bad luck; it's an example of bad statistics and bad science. Improbabilities such as these properly belong to the realm of Douglas Adams.

Were these claimed 25-standard deviation events unique, it would be possible to gloss over the inconsistencies between real life and theoretical forecasts, but in finance statistical impossibilities are quite literally an everyday occurrence. Each and every day financial markets move in ways that simply cannot be explained by our theories of how these markets work.

Nevertheless, despite overwhelming evidence to the contrary, the Efficient Market Hypothesis remains the bedrock of how conventional wisdom views the financial system, the key premise upon which we conduct monetary policy and the framework on which we construct our financial risk systems.

1.7 We Already Have A Better Theory

Fortunately, there is an alternative theory of how financial markets operate, one that is fully able to explain the credit crunch we are now witnessing, and one that, with a little thought, can also explain the erratic behaviour of financial markets. The theory in question is the Financial Instability Hypothesis, developed by the American economist

Hyman P Minsky. Minsky himself credited many of his ideas to another great economist John Maynard Keynes, whose famous 1936 book "The General Theory of Employment, Interest and Money" provided a comprehensive refutation of the idea of efficient markets.

Among my collection of obscure and unfashionable economics books I have one written, in 1975, by Hyman Minsky titled simply "John Maynard Keynes". My copy of this book, which is now out of print, is stamped on the top, bottom and inside cover, with the words 'DISCARDED' in bright red letters. According to its markings the book comes from the Erie City & County Library, Pennsylvania, where it sat largely unread since 1977.

Discarded is a fair way to describe how the finance and economics communities have, up until very recently, treated Minsky's Financial Instability Hypothesis and Keynes' refutation of efficient market theory. For now, conventional wisdom remains with the Efficient Market Hypothesis; however, this latest financial turmoil has shaken at least some of the faithful and the term "Minsky Moment" has now made its way into the popular press as a phrase describing the point at which a credit cycle suddenly turns from expansion to contraction.

In the following chapters I hope to bring some of Minsky's wisdom to a wider audience and show how the processes he identified fall easily into agreement with the behaviour of real financial markets.[6] At the same time I aim to highlight some of the logical inconsistencies in what passes for today's conventional wisdom on matters of macroeconomic policy, while also explaining how these inconsistencies have resulted in dangerously destabilising monetary policy.

---

[6] While I believe I have stuck to the spirit of Minsky's message I have not slavishly followed the details of how he presented his arguments, which are at times unnecessarily technical for a wider audience. I should also note that many of the essentials of Minsky's theory had already been presented by Irving Fisher in 1933 and, according to Minsky, also by Keynes in 1936.

1.8 Internal Or External?

The key difference between the Efficient Market Hypothesis and Minsky's Financial Instability Hypothesis comes down to the question of what makes the prices within financial markets move. As discussed, efficient market theory says that markets move naturally only toward equilibrium, and after reaching equilibrium they remain in this quiescent state until influenced by a new, unexpected, *external* event. The emphasis here is on the external nature of the force causing financial markets to move. By contrast, Minsky's Instability Hypothesis argues that financial markets can generate their own internal forces, causing waves of credit expansion and asset inflation followed by waves of credit contraction and asset deflation.

The implications of Minsky's suggestion are that financial markets are not self-optimising, or stable, and certainly do not lead toward a natural optimal resource allocation. In short, Minsky's arguments attack the very foundation of today's laissez-faire economic orthodoxy, as did those of Keynes before him.

Answering the question of whether or not Minsky is correct boils down to the challenge of identifying processes, internal to the financial markets, which may build upon themselves becoming strong enough to push the markets away from any given equilibrium position. If processes such as these can be identified, then the Efficient Market Hypothesis must be rejected and with it today's accepted wisdom on how to conduct macroeconomic policy.

Two internally-generated destabilising forces have already been introduced in the form of: supply, or the lack thereof, as a driver of demand in asset markets; and asset price changes as a driver of asset demand. The bulk of the rest of the book will follow Minsky's lead and focus on explaining the much more powerful destabilising forces generated within the banking system and the credit creation process broadly.

1.9 Money Market Funds – A Banking System In Miniature

In the US, money market mutual funds are a common feature of the financial landscape. Many of these funds are what is known as "stable-dollar" funds, and are constructed to mimic the behaviour of traditional bank current accounts.

To investors, these stable-dollar money market funds appear to walk and talk like any ordinary bank account. Cash can be paid into, and withdrawn from, the funds on a daily basis, and any holdings within the fund accrue interest each day. As with any bank account, investors in stable-dollar money market funds expect to get back the money they have paid into the fund *plus* interest. As for bank accounts, where it is considered unacceptable to lose or fail to repay a depositor's money on demand, in these funds also losses, or the failure to return an investor's cash on demand, are considered unacceptable.

The object of stable-dollar money market funds is to provide its investors with a rate of interest usually available only on longer-term deposit accounts, while at the same time giving investors instant access to their cash.[7]

---

[7] In the money markets it is normal to receive higher rates of interest when committing to deposit funds for longer periods. Typically savers wanting instant access to their cash will receive the lowest rates of interest while those willing to deposit money for a few months at a time will receive a higher interest rate. The interest rates offered even on deposits of just a few months are often substantially higher than overnight rates.

1.9.1 Stable dollar US money market funds – as banks

The little bit of financial alchemy which gives investors both high interest and instant access to their cash works as follows: many small individual investors treat the fund like a bank deposit account, making small deposits and withdrawals each day. On most days the investors' deposits and withdrawals more or less cancel each other out, leaving the fund's overall assets roughly unchanged from one day to the next. The individual investors see constantly moving streams of money, whereas the fund manager sees a largely stagnant, and therefore investable, pool of money. The managers are able to use the statistical averaging of the fund's flows for the benefit of the fund's investors.

Usually only a small fraction of the fund's balance is ever in active use at any one time. This fraction is kept at hand to meet the ebb and flow of the investors' deposits and withdrawals. The rest of the money is lent out through the commercial money markets, typically for several months at a time. By lending the money for longer periods the fund manager is able to earn higher interest rates for the clients of the fund. As a result the shareholders enjoy both instant access to their funds and the higher interest rates of term deposits.[8] This all works fine until the moment comes when a large number of investors decide to ask for their money back at the same time.

1.9.2 Conflicted objectives

Each day these funds calculate the average interest rate earned on all of their loans, and from these calculations work out what rate of interest the funds can afford to pay their investors. These rates are available for the funds' investors and potential investors to inspect on a daily basis.

---

[8] To be precise they enjoy higher term deposit rates only on that fraction of the fund's money that the manager feels comfortable in investing for longer periods, though this is typically more than 90% of the fund's assets.

The US money market fund business is an intensely competitive industry, producing a constant pressure on fund managers to offer the best possible interest rates. Those funds consistently offering uncompetitive interest rates quickly find their investors withdrawing their cash and placing it into competitor funds offering higher rates.

In money markets, as with most debt markets, the way to earn the highest rates of interest is to make loans for the longest possible periods to the lowest quality, least-reliable investors. The pressure for high money market yields therefore encourages fund managers toward a high-risk lending strategy. But this strategy runs into direct conflict with the money market fund's commitment to give back all of the investor's money, plus interest earned, without the risk of losses.

1.9.3 An introduction to bank runs

In the event of a loan defaulting within one of these money market funds, the fund manager must calculate the effective interest rate on that particular loan as negative – in effect spreading the loss of the loan out over the remainder of its original life and allocating that loss proportionately across all of the deposits in the fund. In this way, even small defaults could reduce the fund's average yield considerably, thereby encouraging some investors to withdraw their funds. As a result of these withdrawals the fund manager will be forced to reallocate the losses across the now smaller pool of remaining investors. The loyal investors will then suffer an even lower interest rate, which in turn will cause further investor defections and a still heavier allocation of losses to the remaining truly faithful investors. What may have started as a minor default, affecting only a tiny fraction of the fund's assets, can quickly spiral into a self-fulfilling cycle of withdrawals. The end result of which is to leave the last few investors holding all of the losses – in financial markets loyalty frequently does not pay.

The potential for a minor credit default to snowball into the collapse of an entire fund is an example of an inherent instability generated when an institution tries to combine the incompatible objectives of guaranteeing to return an investor's capital, while, at the same time, putting that capital at risk.

I have described this destabilising process with reference to money market mutual funds; however, this problem is common to the entire deposit-taking banking system. The recent crises at the British Northern Rock bank and the US Bear Stearns bank followed the same self-reinforcing pattern of deposit withdrawals. These institutions, as all banks do, had taken in deposits, promised to repay those deposits on demand, but at the same time lent out the deposits, sometimes for as long as thirty years, in the form of risky loans. Once depositors began to suspect that the banks were suffering losses, and that other depositors may already be ahead of them in withdrawing their money, a bank run was triggered.[9]

This basic conflict between guaranteeing return of capital while also putting that capital at risk is a key channel through which financial instability can be, and recently has been, generated. Bank runs flagrantly violate the Efficient Market Hypothesis, and yet neither mainstream economic nor financial market theory make any attempt to integrate these processes into their models of market behaviour.

---

[9] Technically the failure of Northern Rock was caused not by actual defaults but by the fear of future defaults, causing both retail investors and the commercial money market lenders to refuse to lend to the bank.

1.10 Memory And Risk

The existence of bank runs have been well understood in finance for hundreds of years, yet their presence is entirely ignored by financial theory, and, therefore, by financial risk systems. In mathematical terms they can be modelled using what is known as a positive feedback process. Positive feedback systems are those in which an event at one time causes more of that same event to occur in the immediate future; investors withdrawing money today cause more investors to withdraw money tomorrow.

Positive feedback processes require current and future events to be influenced by history, that is to say they exhibit a form of memory. The ability or inability of past events to influence future events provides another way of characterising the difference between the Efficient Market Hypothesis and the Financial Instability Hypothesis. As will be explained later, an essential element of the Efficient Market Hypothesis is the idea that the next move in an asset's price must be entirely random and therefore uninfluenced by any previous price movement. It is this property that allows financial analysts to build estimates of probability distributions of future asset price movements. In turn, these probability distributions permit the development of the quantitative financial risk systems on which banks, analysts, ratings agencies and regulators now rely.

If, in contrast to the principles of market efficiency, financial markets do exhibit a form of memory-driven behaviour, and have even a slight tendency to repeat recent actions, these quantitative risk systems will systematically under-represent the true risks in the financial system. Put differently, building financial risk systems on the premise of the Efficient Market Hypothesis requires these systems to ignore the possibility of scenarios like bank runs. That is to say, our risk systems may be inherently designed to work only when they are not required.

2

Efficient Markets *And* Central Banks?

'There have been three great inventions since the beginning of time: fire, the wheel and central banking.'

Will Rogers, American humorist and social commentator, 1879 – 1935

2.1 Central Banks – Everyone Has One

Every modern economy has a central bank. America has the Federal Reserve System, Great Britain the Bank of England, Europe the newly-formed European Central Bank, and Japan the Bank of Japan. These central banks are amongst the most powerful institutions in the modern world. Their actions determine the interest we earn on our bank accounts and the cost of our mortgages. Indirectly, they influence the value of our homes, our pensions and the cost of our weekly groceries. Their policy decisions are able to generate economic expansions or recessions. They dictate our employment prospects, and can even sway the outcome of elections.

When administered correctly, central bank policy can enhance economic performance, lifting the living standards of all citizens. When managed incorrectly, the central banks have the ability to trigger economic recession, deflation, stagflation, financial turmoil or, as we see today in Zimbabwe, or in Germany in the 1920s, hyperinflation with its associated economic and social collapse.

Given the influence of the central banks, it is no exaggeration to say that the governors of these institutions wield more control over our everyday lives than all but the most senior of our elected politicians. Despite this power, central bankers remain remote from the checks and balances of a democratic system. Nowhere in the world are central bank governors directly elected by the population, and once appointed to their positions, they usually go out of their way to distance themselves from political influence. Today, placing the management of a country's central bank beyond the control of elected government is considered one of the prerequisites of a modern successful capitalist economy.

In recent years there has been a growing popular awareness of the importance of central banking to our economic well-being. The interest rate decisions of central banks are now routinely reported on our evening news shows, and frequently dominate the business pages of our newspapers. Teams of financial analysts use even the most banal utterances of senior central bank officials as an excuse to convert perfectly good trees into mountains of sometimes less-than-useful reports.[10] Bank traders and fund managers, including those looking after our pensions, risk billions of dollars betting on how the central banks will adjust policy in the future, and even, at times, on how they will adjust the tone of their speeches.

2.2 An Expanse Of Confusion

Despite the importance of these institutions, and the intense scrutiny under which they operate, the central banks are still very poorly understood. Few people know why central banks move interest rates, or can explain the importance of their independence from political control. Even within the community of finance professionals and economists, surprisingly few can explain why central banks exist at all. Fewer still can articulate what makes good or bad central bank policy.

2.3 Opinions Differ

Being ignorant of the methods and purpose of central banks is a forgivable sin; even the central bankers themselves disagree on what they are trying to achieve and how they should go about it. Today the two most powerful central banks are the US Federal Reserve System and the EU's European Central Bank. These two institutions both profess to share the common goal of achieving price stability. However,

---

[10] Mea culpa.

this public agreement conceals a deep divide over how to pursue their common objective. The ECB insists that money-supply targeting must play a central role in formulating policy; at their monthly press conferences ECB officials earnestly report the latest M3 figures,[11] recording the rate of monetary expansion within the European Union. Invariably they then go on to insist that these figures must guide their decisions over how and when to move interest rates; too much money supply growth and rates must go up, too little and they should come down. On the other side of the Atlantic, in the offices of the US Federal Reserve, the philosophy could not be more different, where it has been decided that the M3 data is so useless as to be no longer even worth recording, and certainly should not be used as a guide to policy.[12] Controlling monetary policy is the job of central banking, but the central bankers cannot agree on what changing money supply means. The failure to agree on the role of money supply growth in central bank policy is a symptom of the prevailing wisdom within the economics profession having profoundly failed to comprehend the purpose of central banking. As will be explained, the incomprehension arises through an unquestioning faith in the idea of market efficiency.

Having spent more than a decade analysing the policies of central banks on both sides of the Atlantic, I believe the key elements of the differences in strategy between the Federal Reserve and the ECB can be expressed as follows.

---

[11] The M3 figures refer to what is called the rate of money supply growth, which will be explained in more detail in the following chapter. For now just note that whereas "money supply growth" has a reassuring ring to it – more money cannot be a bad thing – it does not mean just more money, it also means more debt. The M3 figures are also measuring the growth rate of our indebtedness. Much of the fog of confusion surrounding macro finance would be lifted if these numbers were to be reported under the more chilling moniker of "debt supply growth".

[12] To be fair to the Fed, they correctly point out that much of the information contained in the M3 figures is also captured by other measures of money supply growth. That said, these other measures are also disregarded.

The US Federal Reserve does not appear to believe there can be an excessive level of money growth, credit creation or asset inflation. They do, however, believe there can be an unacceptably low level of all these variables. As a result, the Fed's monetary policy can be characterised as one in which policy is used aggressively to prevent or reverse credit contraction or asset price deflation, but is not used to prevent credit expansion or asset inflation. This philosophy has been encapsulated by the idea that asset bubbles cannot be identified until after they burst, and it is only then that the central banks can and should take action.

The ECB, by contrast, appears to believe that money supply growth can become excessive; this is consistent with excessive credit creation and is also consistent with asset inflation being excessive. However, there is general reluctance to acknowledge the connection between excessive money supply growth and excessive asset price inflation.

The upshot of these different world views is that the Fed sees its role as combating any credit contraction, whereas the ECB sees its role as combating excessive credit expansion. Doubtless I will have offended sensibilities on both sides of the Atlantic in emphasising differences in the respective monetary policies in such stark terms, while ignoring many areas of broad agreement. For this I apologise; however, the differences in monetary policy strategy are an important part of the story of this and previous credit crises and deserve to be aired.[13]

2.4 Should We Even Have Central Banks?

Focussing first on arguments over how central banks operate risks neglecting an even more interesting conundrum: Why do central banks

---

[13] See "Asset Price Bubbles and Monetary Policy", a speech given in June 2005 by Jean-Claude Trichet, President of the ECB, which touches on some of the issues discussed in this book. http://www.ecb.int/press/key/date/2005/html/sp050608.en.html.

exist at all? Central banks use interest rate policy to control the capital markets. Yet economic theory tells us markets are efficient and should be left to their own devices. Why then do we need central bankers to set interest rates? Surely, we should be able to trust the markets to determine interest rates without recourse to some soviet-style central planning of the capital markets.

It is a strange paradox that today's central banks are generally staffed by economists, who by and large profess a belief in a theory which says their jobs are, at the very best, unnecessary and more likely wealth-destroying. Needless to say, this is not a point widely discussed between respectable economists. Nevertheless, it is an issue worth pondering.

If central banks are necessary because of an inherent instability in financial markets, then manning these institutions with efficient market disciples is a little like putting a conscientious objector in charge of the military; the result will be a state of perpetual unreadyness.

2.5 Efficient Market Hypothesis – Is Flipping Coins

Fortunately, the Efficient Market Hypothesis gives us a way to check its own validity. We have already touched on this topic earlier with the discussion of the fat-tails problem, but it is worth giving it a little more consideration now.

The efficient market story goes as follows. All asset prices are currently at their correct level. If we were able to reliably predict how any asset price were likely to move in the future, we would be able to reliably make a profit from buying or selling that asset. But if it were possible to reliably make a profit through buying or selling the asset then that asset's current price must be wrong. Therefore, according to the Efficient Market Hypothesis, asset prices must be unpredictable.

The next step in the story is the masterstroke. Since we cannot reliably predict the direction of the next price movement, it must be equally likely that the next price move is up or down. And since there are only two equally possible directions in which a price may move, the probability of a price increase is 50% and the probability of a price decrease is 50%. According to the Efficient Market Hypothesis these probabilities hold always and everywhere.[14] What's more, if we are to be unable to reliably make profits from these price movements, then the expected magnitude of the moves in each direction must, like their probabilities, be equal.[15]

When we put all of this together we get the marvellous result that asset price movements can be modelled as if they were being controlled by a process no more complicated than flipping a coin: heads the next price movement is up, with a 50% probability; tails the next movement is down, with a 50% probability. This is very fortunate because mathematicians and physicists have already done all of the heavy lifting in working out how things move when controlled by entirely random processes like these.[16]

---

[14] Steady state asset price inflation is frequently added into models of price behaviour in order to bring them a little closer to reality. Such corrections are frequently reasonable given the inflationary bias of monetary policy and a general tendency toward economic growth; however, for the purpose of the current discussion these adjustments can be ignored.

[15] I'm being just a little economical with the truth here. Technically, because asset prices generally cannot become negative, when a price gets close to zero the size of the next possible price decline becomes a little smaller than the size of the next possible price rise. By making this adjustment the normal probability distributions, which are discussed in the rest of this book, become log normal probability distributions. For all practical purposes you can, if you have not already done so, forget this piece of information.

[16] Albert Einstein was awarded his PhD for developing the mathematics explaining random walks, or Brownian motion, these being the paths followed by particles, and supposedly asset prices, when subjected to a procession of entirely random shocks.

As it turns out, if assets prices follow entirely random processes, moving up and down in a series of tiny steps, then provided we allow enough steps the whole procedure can be simulated with what are called normal or Gaussian probability distributions.

Convincing ourselves that the probability distribution of asset price movements can be considered as normal distributions is convenient because these distributions are very easy to work with. When using normal distributions we need only a single number to permit us to forecast the entire probability distribution of future asset returns. The number we need is essentially a measure of how spread out the distribution is and is known as the standard deviation. Intuitively, this is equivalent to asking how big the random steps are on average; big steps imply a very spread out distribution with a wide range of possible asset returns, implying a large standard deviation.

2.6 Coin Flipping And Volatility – Foundations Of The Options Industry

Now that the Efficient Market Hypothesis has yielded us a perfectly defined shape for an asset's return distribution, all that is left is to calibrate the width of the distribution. Calibrating the width of these probability distributions is done by measuring the standard deviation of the asset price's previous moves. Essentially, we measure the average size of the previous random price jumps and hope the same pattern of price movements will be repeated in the future, which according to the Efficient Market Hypothesis should hold true.

Once this calibration step is performed we supposedly know the entire possible future return distribution, spanning all eventualities; we know its shape – derived from theory – and its range – derived from history.

This breakthrough in asset price modelling opens up a wealth of possibilities. Banks, asset managers, insurance companies, regulators, anyone at all who needs to worry about financial risk can use these distributions to work out their probability of losses. From this discovery it was only a small step toward the development of the options industry, which effectively slices and dices these distributions, selling the different parts to different investors. Conservative investors may choose to buy insurance against the bottom portion of the return distribution, protecting their portfolio against losses, while more aggressive, and optimistic, investors may choose to sell that portion of the distribution.

2.7 Testing The Hypothesis

The fact that the Efficient Market Hypothesis can be converted into these neat known-probability distributions gives us a method to check if the theory is correct. If markets are efficient, then over time we should be able to record data on asset price changes, collect that data into realised return distributions, and compare the real distributions with those which had been previously forecast. In this way we should be able to establish if the statistical predictions of efficient market theory are supported by evidence. These tests have been done time and again across all conceivable asset markets allowing us to build up a picture of asset price returns that unequivocally fails to support the Efficient Market Hypothesis.

While Bear Stearns and Northern Rock corroborate the failure of efficient market theory, the best demonstration of the problem comes in the story of the hedge fund Long Term Capital Management. To quote Roger Lowenstein:

The heart of the fund was a group of brainy, Ph.D.-certified arbitrageurs. Many of them had been professors. Two had won the Nobel Prize. All of them were very smart.[17]

The LTCM fund was staffed by the crème de la crème of those that had been responsible for developing the Efficient Market Hypothesis. Yet why were these Nobel prize winners, who had won their awards for theories based directly on the Efficient Market Hypothesis, wasting their time in a company whose purpose it was to predict the supposedly unpredictable financial markets?

Had LTCM just failed to make money the Efficient Market Hypothesis would have been untarnished, but this is not what happened. First, LTCM made spectacular profits, quadrupling its net asset value steadily over a four-year period. Then, in just a few weeks, it lost all and more of the previous gains. LTCM managed to disprove the Efficient Market Hypothesis in two ways; first by making profits that should not have been available, and then by incurring losses as the result of sudden massive market movements which should also not have been possible.

The story of the LTCM was as if Albert Einstein had partnered with Richard Feynman in order to disprove their own theories of physics. That they had succeeded, but then the world had gone on as if nothing had happened, still believing the disproven theories.

---

[17] See page xix of "When Genius Failed" by Roger Lowenstein, who recounts the colourful tale of the failure of LTCM and in so doing provides an excellent real life example of the inadequacy of the Efficient Market Hypothesis.

2.8 Time To Take Stock

The idea that markets are efficient requires the following to hold:

1. Asset price bubbles do not exist; the prices of all assets are always correct.

2. Markets, when left alone, will converge to a steady equilibrium state.

3. That equilibrium state will be the optimum state.

4. Individual asset price movements are unpredictable.

5. However, the distributions of asset price movements are predictable.

The only fly in the ointment of this grand story is, as noted, the data just doesn't fit the theory. We don't find normally-distributed markets; we do find huge market discontinuities and, let's be honest, a static stable equilibrium has never once been observed anywhere in financial markets.[18]

2.9 Disproving One Theory *Should* Lead To A Better Theory

So we've got ourselves into something of a pickle with the Efficient Market Hypothesis. We've polished it into a well-honed economic philosophy of laissez-faire, and we've also refined it into a testable theory of financial market behaviour, and then we have found that it fails its own tests.

---

[18] Probably the closest thing to an equilibrium that has been observed within the financial system is the prolonged period of depressed activity of the Great Depression in the 1930s. But this equilibrium could in no way be described as an optimal equilibrium.

At this point, crushed by the overwhelming burden of contradictory data, the scientific response would be to throw in the towel, abandon the fairy tale of market efficiency and look for a better theory. This is the path taken by Keynes when, in the 1930s, he observed that the Great Depression did not show economies moving toward the optimal equilibrium state, causing him to develop a new economic theory which rejected the idea of market efficiency.[19] It is also what Minsky did with his Financial Instability Hypothesis.[20] Attacking a different facet of the same problem, this is also what the mathematician Benoit Mandelbrot – famous for fractal geometry and the Mandelbrot set – has done in developing alternative models of market behaviour to those suggested by random Brownian motion.[21]

2.10 Two Schools Or The Mad House

While Keynes, and then Minsky, set out in one direction to formulate a new alternative theory of how the world works, which fitted with the experimental evidence, another group set out in the opposite direction, determined to rescue the idea of market efficiency and the all-important doctrine of laissez-faire that accompanies it.

---

[19] See "The General Theory of Employment Interest and Money" by John Maynard Keynes, 1936. Keynes's work has been widely interpreted as a multiple equilibrium theory, one that permits markets to, at times, find the best equilibrium and, at other times, to find a sub-optimal equilibrium.

[20] See "Stabilizing an Unstable Economy" by Hyman Minsky, 1986. Minsky's work is not a multiple equilibrium theory but rather a no-equilibrium theory. Broadly speaking, Minsky suggests that financial systems do not settle down into a stable state, and instead have two states of basically expanding or contracting credit. Minsky's model allows the economy to generate its own irregular cycles.

[21] See "Fractals and Scaling in Finance" by Benoit B. Mandelbrot. Mandelbrot finds evidence of markets behaving as if they had memory, driven by previous events. He also finds evidence of sharp price movements clustering together. Mandelbrot's ideas, I believe, dovetail with those of Minsky's Financial Instability Hypothesis.

This second team has a different explanation for why market behaviour fails to fit with the Efficient Market Hypothesis. One of the conditions for markets to operate efficiently is that they be left alone, free to operate without interference or manipulation. If market prices are pushed around and manipulated by external forces, for example by government interference, then the markets cannot be expected to behave as efficient markets should. The "get out of jail free card" for the Efficient Market Hypothesis comes from noting that financial markets are not free markets but are heavily manipulated by government and especially central bank interference. This leads to an intriguing possibility: that boom-bust asset price cycles and non-normal return distributions are not due to some inherent failure of the markets, but are instead the result of central bank interference.

2.10.1 The Friedman school – central banks make markets inefficient

If one subscribes to the Efficient Market Hypothesis and also happens to be cursed by intellectual rigour, the unavoidable conclusion is that central banks should be abolished. If markets are self-optimising, then free market forces should be allowed to set interest rates. Banks should be permitted to lend and borrow on whatever terms they deem appropriate, guided only by the market forces of the supply and demand for capital.

It may come as a surprise to many to discover that this was the position of Milton Friedman, one of the world's foremost monetary economists, who believed central banks distorted financial markets and should be abolished. In an interview shortly before his death in November 2006, Friedman was asked: '...would it be preferable to abolish the Fed entirely and just have government stick to a monetary growth rule?' Friedman replied: 'Yes, it's preferable, and there's no chance at all of it happening.'[22] Friedman's position on central banking looks radical, but then so was Einstein's on gravity.

When properly thought through, Friedman's position was not the result of radical thought at all; it was just the logical and honest progression that must follow from a belief in efficient markets. Today's economic orthodoxy parrots Friedman's reverence of free markets, but does not apply his intellectual rigour in extrapolating what efficient markets imply about the role of central banking.

The current political orthodoxy is in a similarly schizophrenic state. The rigorous application of market forces to the management of state-controlled institutions is now universally presented as the path to better governance. Despite this, almost no one has thought to apply these market principles to central banks and to the determination of interest rates. One politician, however, has made the logical connection; the US Congressman, and one-time 2008 presidential candidate, Ron Paul, has like Friedman arrived at a view of central banking consistent with free market principles. In 2002, Paul introduced legislation aiming to abolish of the US Federal Reserve. Paul's objective was to return the US to a gold standard, which was the monetary system in operation prior to 1971.

Both Friedman and Paul's concerns over central banks are similar. Both cite the inherently inflationary bias of a fiat money system (see chapter 3) when placed in the hands of a government bureaucracy, and both cite the potential for misguided policy actions causing destabilising boom-bust cycles. (Gold standards, inflation and the stability of banking systems are the subject of the next chapter.)

---

[22] Quoted from an interview with *Reason* magazine "Can we Bank on the Federal Reserve" November 2006, http://www.reason.com/news/show/38384.html.

The Friedman/Paul position is appealing for its intellectual clarity in that it offers an explanation for why today's financial market data does not fit today's financial market theories. Certainly the current credit crisis, coupled with surging oil and commodity prices, lend weight to the warnings of over boom-bust cycles and inflation.

2.10.2 The Keynes/Minsky school – markets are inefficient, central banks make them more efficient[23]

The alternate viewpoint is that markets are not fundamentally stable or self-optimising, and as a result require oversight and management. Both Keynes and Minsky emphasised the government's role in providing this management through state spending and fiscal measures. Central banking can be viewed in the same way as these fiscal measures, as being a necessary part of, in Minsky's words, 'stabilising an unstable economy'.

As with Friedman's position, the Keynes/Minsky perspective is attractive for its intellectual consistency in that it fits with real financial market behaviour and with the real institutions operating in our economies. While both the Friedman and the Keynes schools are logical they cannot both be correct; to one central banks cause financial instability, to the other they cure it.

2.10.3 The mad house – markets are efficient and we need central banks

Let us step back and consider the current state of affairs from the proverbial 60,000-foot perspective. The world is currently in the grip

---

[23] Keynes did argue for a centralised management of the credit creation process, though here I am using the term Keynes/Minsky School to refer broadly to the idea that market systems and economies require managing, rather than to a specific view expressed on central bank policy.

of a credit crunch, possibly the largest in history. We have one philosophy of economics and finance that tells us these crises shouldn't happen and can be avoided, provided we stop tinkering with the economy and shut down our central banks. We have another philosophy that says these crises are inherent in the system and we need central banks to help manage them.

Then there is a third school, which also happens to be today's conventional wisdom, which is a confused mishmash of ideas drawn from both camps. This school professes to believe in efficient markets and in the necessity of central banks; it is, however, unable to articulate a coherent description of what central banks are for or how they should operate. Unfortunately, some of the world's most powerful central banks are operated according to the confused position of this third school.

2.11 Is This Science?

In cycle after cycle the same script is acted out. An asset bubble begins inflating, together with its associated credit bubble. The lead singers of the free market school strike up their familiar song: markets know best, markets are efficient, there are no bubbles, let the markets run. While asset prices rise and credit expands, the doctrine of market efficiency reigns supreme. But immediately as asset prices begin falling and the credit bubble begins contracting, the singers swiftly change tune. The free-marketeers cast aside their message and, without even the decency to blush, strike up a new song: central banks must cut rates, governments must stimulate, credit must not contract, asset prices must not be allowed to fall. While the lead singers flip from song to song, apparently unaware of their discordant lyrics, the backing singers maintain a constant comical chant: markets are stable, markets are stable, markets are stable.

We are asked to subscribe to one economic philosophy for an expanding economy and another quite incompatible philosophy for a contracting economy. The presence of financial instability, clear for all the world to see, is ignored, and the function of central banks goes entirely unexplained.

For a field of study aspiring to the status of a science today's economic consensus is in a risible state, both internally inconsistent and entirely in conflict with the experimental evidence. Had Isaac Newton subjected himself to these same standards he would have given us three laws of gravity: one telling us how an apple behaves when thrown up into the air; another quite different law telling us how it then falls back to earth; and a third law telling us the apple never moves at all.

2.12 In Summary

Our economic theories tell us that financial markets are stable and never mis-priced; experience shows this to be patently untrue. Efficient market theories tell us that central banks are unnecessary; most economists tell us efficient market theories are correct and central banks are necessary, but cannot explain why. Some central banks think money supply is important to monetary policy while others think money supply is unimportant for monetary policy.

Today the general consensus is that the central banks have made mistakes and inadvertently created the conditions leading up to the current credit crisis. Sadly, when we turn to the economic orthodoxy for an opinion on what went wrong and how we can fix it we find there is not even an established framework by which we can discuss the issue.

Before we can work out what, if anything, has gone wrong with central bank policy in the run-up to this crisis we first have to work out what monetary policy should do. First though, before we can even get to this question, we have to work out whether central banks should exist at all.

If the Friedman school is correct and financial markets are destabilised by the presence of central banks, then today's events suggest we should shut down these institutions forthwith.

If the Keynes/Minsky school is correct and markets are inefficient and unstable and require stabilising by central banks, then we must work out what it is that led to the failure of these stabilising policies of late, and how to implement better policies in the future.

To avoid unnecessary suspense, the next chapter argues the Efficient Market Hypothesis is flawed beyond redemption, financial markets are pathologically unstable, and central banks are a vital part of our financial architecture. The subsequent chapters then argue that, in some central banks, a misguided loyalty to the idea of market efficiency is leading to policies that inadvertently amplify rather than attenuate market instability.

3

Money, Banks And Central Banks

'The process by which banks create money is so simple that the mind is repelled.'

John Kenneth Galbraith

'Bank failures are caused by depositors who don't deposit enough money to cover the losses due to mismanagement.'

Dan Quayle

3.1 The ECB's Inflation Monster

The website of the European Central Bank (ECB) contains a section of educational material devoted to teaching children about the role of central banking and the evils of inflation. One of the items on the site is a short animated movie. The movie's story begins in a classroom with a teacher explaining the ECB's definition of price stability to her pupils:[24]

> Today we are going to talk about price stability. Price stability as defined by the governing council of the European Central Bank is the year-on-year increase in the harmonized index of consumer prices for the Euro area of below two percent...

The teacher drones on and, understandably, the children start drifting off to sleep. At this point two of the children find themselves transported back in time, standing in the centre of what appears to be a busy medieval market square. The children approach the market stall of the town baker (for some reason it's always a baker in stories like these) whereupon they try to buy some cakes.

To the children's dismay, they find that each time they attempt to pay the baker for his cakes he suddenly raises his prices. The baker explains that this is because the price of firewood and corn keep rising. At this point the children turn around and are confronted by a rather friendly-looking Inflation Monster. This dastardly Inflation Monster then proceeds to force money upon the two hapless children, and to make matters worse continues his fiendish work by scattering even more money across the market square.

---

[24] http://www.ecb.int/ecb/educational/pricestab/html/index.en.html.

The children soon learn that the source of the inflation in the price of the baker's cakes is the money being scattered around by the Inflation Monster. Too much money, chasing too few goods, causes inflation they are told. A few moments later they find themselves transported back to the present day, sitting in the offices of no less an institution than the European Central Bank itself. The children meet a smiling European Central banker who proceeds to lecture them about monetary stability, credit creation and interest rates. Toward the end of the lecture the central banker produces a glass jar from under his desk with the Inflation Monster safely trapped inside it. The not-so subliminal message being: inflation was a thing of the past, but now we've got it contained.

Fortunately for the children they are released from the grip of the grinning central banker and, in the final scene, are transported back to their classroom, fully educated about inflation.

As cartoons go it is actually quite well made and certainly worth the eight minutes it takes to watch. But as an educational piece of about inflation what it omits is at least as interesting as what it contains. There is one little white lie: the Inflation Monster is presented as existing in historical times, presumably while the gold standard was in operation, but having been captured in the present day. And there is one glaring omission: no explanation is given for why a beast such as the Inflation Monster would ever give away money for free. In an economy governed by efficient markets: Why do we have an Inflation Monster giving away money?

One should not be too harsh on the cartoon's scriptwriters; presentational slip-ups like these are common fare in the world of economics. Today, central bankers like to portray themselves as the warriors of a never-ending war against inflation. Inflation, they would have us believe, is an ever-present danger lurking somewhere within the economy, a danger requiring constant vigilance, sometimes even extreme vigilance. Where this Inflation Monster comes from, and why he performs the dastardly act of giving away money, goes unexplained.

3.2 The Inflation Monster And The Efficient Market Hypothesis

When we start looking for an explanation for inflation we run once more into our old friend the Efficient Market Hypothesis. Recall Samuelson's passage, from the start of the first chapter, telling us that markets were efficient because they were competitive. According to the Efficient Market Hypothesis, competition between suppliers for customers should automatically ensure price competition, thereby keeping inflation in check. Indeed, if we were to stretch the argument a little further, we could easily conclude that deflation, or disinflation, should be the normal state of affairs: competition should spur manufacturers to seek more efficient production methods, allowing them to make goods at lower cost, and competitive forces should ensure that, over time, those lower costs are passed on to the consumer. QED – efficient markets are consistent with disinflation, not inflation.

Whatever the theory might say, inflation is without doubt still present in our economic system to a greater or lesser degree. Personally, I have yet to be handed any free money by the Inflation Monster and know of no other person who has come across the mythical beast – though I still live in hope. Nor can I imagine any conceivable free market process that would conjure an Inflation Monster into being. Once again we have another glaring hole in today's economic parable: the efficient market model can explain neither inflation nor central banking – and there may just be a link between these two mysteries.

3.3 Hunting The Monster: A Brief (Partially Fictional) History of Money

To hunt down the Inflation Monster, and to understand how it evolved, it is necessary to know a little about the history of money. Unfortunately most histories of money get distracted on the details of Pacific islanders swapping seashells, prisoners-of-war trading cigarettes, or the artistic merit of ancient Persian coinage. These histories are interesting as histories but are of little help in understanding how today's financial system works. For this reason, in the following section I have made up a fictional history of money to convey something of how we arrived at our current monetary system, the key elements of the system, and how the Inflation Monster came into being.

3.3.1 Barter exchange

Long, long ago, the first trade was conducted via barter. All goods were exchanged directly for all other goods. It wasn't a great system; if you wanted to swap your chicken for a loaf of bread, but the baker happened to want firewood, you were stuck with the task of traipsing around the market square until you could find someone with firewood who just happened to want a chicken. Despite its drawbacks we muddled along with barter exchange for a few hundred thousand years. Unsurprisingly, this period was not one of rapid economic growth.

Growth may have been lacking but at least financial instability was not a problem. All goods were exchanged for each other in real time; no finance means no financial instability. In the barter exchange economy there is no sign of an Inflation Monster; no one would scatter valuable chickens around a marketplace for free.

3.3.2 Gold exchange

The first big breakthrough in finance came when everyone agreed that barter exchange was just taking too long. Under the new system everyone agreed to accept gold in return for whatever they were selling. This transition allowed the swapping of chickens for gold and then gold for anything else – the baker could jolly well find his own firewood.

Once gold took on the role of a recognised means of exchange it also inadvertently became a store of value. If in one season you happened to have a lot of chickens, you could swap all of the chickens for gold, spend only part of the gold on bread, and keep a few nuggets for a rainy day.

Money becoming a store of value was the start of monetary inflation cycles and a prototype of financial instability. If you happened to have too many chickens this season, the chances were so would all the other chicken sellers. If everyone tried to sell at the same time, there would be too many chickens chasing too little gold and pretty soon you'd have chicken deflation, or gold inflation depending on your perspective.

The emergence of gold's secondary function as a store of value allowed demand to be transferred through time. Under a gold exchange system there would certainly have been inflation and deflation cycles, sometimes within specific goods and sometimes more generally, most likely linked to harvests, wars, disease and the like. However, these would have been cycles, that is to say prices would have gone up and then down, but on average stayed more or less the same over very long periods.[25]

---

[25] In the interest of clarity I have missed out some important details, not least the demographic effects on inflation in history. For those interested in a more complete picture, "The Great Wave, Price Revolutions and the Rhythm of History" by David H. Fischer makes for fascinating reading.

At this stage we could get price cycles but there is no systematic trend toward higher prices, and there is certainly no sign of any Inflation Monster randomly scattering nuggets across the marketplace.

3.3.3 Gold money (coins)

Economically speaking, the step from gold exchange to gold coins was evolutionary rather than revolutionary. The main breakthrough was the agreement to divide the gold up into uniform manageable lumps of equal weight and equal purity.

The invention of coins made trade easier, and encouraged economic expansion. This economic expansion meant that transactions got bigger, so carrying and securing the coins became more troublesome. An annoying habit of coin clipping also emerged, where people would shave gold from the edges of the coins, and turn these clippings into more coins. This was the start of monetary debasement. It took the genius of none other than Isaac Newton to come up with the idea of milling fine lines onto the edges of the coins, making it easier to detect if the coins had been clipped.[26]

While coin clipping was practiced within the private sector, in the state sector monetary debasement took on an industrial scale. Governments, especially when in financial trouble, would recall their coinage, melt it down and reform the metal into more coins with a lower gold content. Private sector coin clipping was a crime punishable by death; public sector coin clipping (recoinage) was considered monetary policy; both caused an increase in the number of coins relative to goods and therefore inflation.

---

[26] Between developing calculus gravity and the laws of motion, Isaac Newton also found time to become master of the Royal Mint, whereupon he introduced new techniques of producing coins to make forgery more difficult.

Needless to say the process of recoinage, whereby the government demanded its population turn over their coins and have them replaced by new worth-less coins, was not a popular procedure. For government, however, it generated a nice new pile of gold for conversion into extra coins for their own coffers.

Recoinage, or debasement, the process of progressively reducing the gold content of coins, represents the conception point for a prototype Inflation Monster. But recoinage was a difficult time-consuming process, which was conducted only occasionally. When it happened there would be a sudden flood of extra money into the system, met by a burst of inflation. However, once the prices had adjusted to the new coinage inflation would stop once more.

Even with recoinage there is still absolutely no sign of the ECB's Inflation Monster throwing away coins in the market square. Recoinage was orchestrated for the purpose of generating extra coins to be thrown in the direction of the government – not given out for free in the market square. The inflationary recoinage engaged in by Newton had much to do with England's budget deficit as a result of it being at war with Europe at the time; the connection between inflation and war financing remains with us to this day. The key point to take away from this is the close connection between taxation and inflation. The two are almost synonymous, with inflation representing a retrospective taxation.

3.3.4 Gold certificates

The next big leap in the development of money was revolutionary and came with the invention of certificates of gold deposits. Debasement, coin clipping and the larger monetary transactions, due to economic expansion, meant that gold coins became difficult to deal with. Each transaction required that the coins be counted, weighed and checked for purity and authenticity. In addition to which there was the constant problem of security; it is presumably quite difficult to conceal a thousand gold sovereigns about your person.

These problems lead to the development of gold depository banks. Groups of merchants got together to form merchant banks that would hold their gold securely at a central location. The quality of the coinage was checked as it was deposited, and the depositor was issued with a paper certificate of deposit. The certificate of deposit represented his holdings of gold within the bank and the holder of this certificate was entitled to present the certificate back to the bank, who would, on demand, exchange it for the same amount of gold coins originally deposited.

On the face of it the development of gold depository banks and the use of gold certificates of deposit, for trade, looked like merely a technical change in how gold was moved between merchants. But this technical change was to lead to an entirely new financial system, and the emergence of modern day financial instability.

The depository banks soon worked out that the merchants who had deposited their gold very rarely came back to collect it. What's more, the small inflows and outflows of gold that did occur tended, on most days, to cancel one another out. As a result the bankers found themselves sitting on a large pile of gold coins, which were mostly idle.

3.3.5 Gold certificates and credit creation

Needless to say, the combination of bankers and large piles of unused money was not a stable equilibrium; after staring at the unused gold for a short while, the bankers soon came up with their own money-making ruse.

The ruse worked as follows. The bankers would issue their own certificates of gold deposit, and would lend those certificates to merchants. These merchants would use the new certificates to buy goods, which they would then sell on at a profit. Provided everything went well, the merchant could borrow the certificate, buy and sell the goods to make the profit, and repay the bank before anyone ever realised that the gold had left the vaults – which of course it never had.

At the end of the chain of events the merchant would be left with the profit from his transactions, which he would split with the bankers, in return for their "interest" in the transaction.

Even if the transaction took a little longer to complete, the bank would not necessarily be in trouble. Were the second merchant, from whom the goods were bought, to present the bank's certificate of deposit and ask for the corresponding amount of gold, the bankers would be able to deliver the gold from their pile of idle reserves. This outflow of gold could then be remedied once the first merchant repaid the original loan.[27]

Let's look at this process a little closer. At outset there are gold coins sitting in the bank, and the same value of gold certificates circulating around the economy in the hands of the merchants that really owned the gold. Then the bank creates another gold certificate, which it gives to another merchant, and this too is circulated into the economy. While the loan is in existence there are more certificates of deposit in circulation than there are gold deposits in the bank. But once the loan is repaid the outstanding certificates are brought back into line with the actual gold reserves.

---

[27] If the loan were repaid with a certificate of deposit from another bank, the bankers could then, if they felt the need, replenish their own gold stock by redeeming this new certificate. Alternatively, if it were one of their own certificates then the outstanding claims against their own gold reserves would have fallen by a little more than the value of the withdrawn gold (once the interest payment is taken into account), which would keep their books balanced.

This process makes two vital contributions to financial instability. The first and most important being that once this system really took hold there were always more certificates of deposit in circulation than there was gold in the vaults of the banks. The depository banks were therefore not in a position to redeem all their outstanding certificates at once.[28] The second contribution to financial instability arose through the mechanism by which loans were opened and closed. The banks would open a loan by issuing their own depository certificate to a merchant, who would in turn issue the bank with his own promissory note, committing to repay the loan. However, in the process of performing his trade the merchant was himself likely to receive payment in the form of a depository certificate from another bank. When this certificate was used to repay the loan, the bank would then be left holding a claim on gold held at another bank. Over time the banks would be left with a spaghetti-like network of interlocking claims against one another.

As the system evolved the amount of bank-generated certificates of deposit eventually came to vastly outnumber those backed by real gold reserves. Therefore, even under the gold standard, the monetary system was predominantly secured on debt.

3.3.6 Banking crises with depository banks

Hopefully, it is easy to see how financial instability could occur within a gold depository system. Imagine, for example, that a loan were used to fund the cargo of a ship, and the ship was then lost at sea. The merchant would have borrowed the certificate of deposit and given it

---

[28] Theoretically all of the outstanding gold certificates could be redeemed only if *all* of the merchants were able to pay off *all* of their loans simultaneously and the banks were then able to net off their respective liabilities to one another.

to another merchant in return for the claim on the ship's cargo. The first merchant would have no hope of repaying the loan, and the second merchant would know this and would also know that he was now holding a certificate of deposit from a bank that was about to suffer a default.

Being a cautious fellow, this second merchant would likely present the note to the bank and ask for his gold. He may even discreetly advise some of his friends to also redeem any certificates they happened to hold from the same bank. The bank in question may have quite sufficient of its own capital to write off the value of the merchant's defaulted loan, but it would not have enough gold in its vaults to redeem all of its outstanding depository certificates. As the word began to spread that merchants were withdrawing physical gold from the bank there will then be a cascade effect, whereby the more gold withdrawn the greater the panic from the remaining certificate holders. In other words the bank would suffer a bank run.

Naturally, in a situation like this, other banks would cease lending to the troubled institution and would also seek to redeem any certificates of deposit that they happened to hold from the bank. For its part, the troubled bank would likewise seek to replenish its coffers by tendering any notes it happened to hold from other banks for conversion into gold while also attempting to recall any loans made to merchants. These merchants would then either have to seek other funds or quickly raise money by selling their goods and assets.

This is not some abstract thought experiment; bank runs of this type can and did happen under the gold standard.[29] What's more, bank runs can

---

[29] "The Moneymaker" by Janet Gleeson chronicles just such an event with the introduction of paper money and fractional reserve banking in France in 1716. If ever there is a finance book worthy of becoming a Hollywood blockbuster it is this one.

and do happen under our current monetary system. At the time of Northern Rock's failure the credit quality of its loan book had showed little if any sign of deterioration. Nevertheless, credit concerns, centred on other institutions, caused lenders to refuse loans to Northern Rock. When news of this got out depositors began to line the streets seeking to withdraw their own funds, making Northern Rock even less able to borrow from other institutions.

3.3.7 Private sector credit creation is not the Inflation Monster

Our search for the Inflation Monster has brought us to one flavour of financial instability, but not yet to the Inflation Monster itself. Even under a banking system with far more certificates of deposit outstanding than reserves in the vaults – fractional reserve banking as it is called[30] – each individual receipt still retained its full theoretical claim to a fixed quantity of gold. There is, therefore, no earthly reason for an Inflation Monster to give away these certificates in any marketplace.

In a period of strong economic performance, when the confidence of bankers is generally improving, one would see the banking system extend more credit. As a result there would be more certificates chasing the same goods, and inflation would result. But the converse would also be true; as confidence fell back the banks would become more cautious, cutting back on their issuance of certificates, money supply would shrink and goods prices would fall back.

The invention of the credit creation system associated with gold depository certificates would have the power to amplify inflation and deflation cycles, but in the end the certificates would be tied to a fixed quantity of gold; price volatility would increase, but there would be no

---

[30] The term "fractional reserve banking" refers to the practice by which banks would retain gold reserves on hand worth just a small fraction of their total outstanding lending.

secular trend toward ever higher prices, such as witnessed in today's economy. We may have found the monster's cousin, but the monster himself still eludes us.

3.3.8 Money and anti-money

Economics has a long tradition of borrowing concepts from the physical sciences; when it comes to *private sector* credit creation there is a useful analogue in the modern theory of quantum physics. The German Nobel Prize-winning Physicist Werner Heisenberg worked out that nature did not always respect the principle of conservation of energy. Prior to Heisenberg's discovery it was believed that energy could never be created or destroyed, but only rearranged. Heisenberg realised that for very short periods of time the law of conservation of energy could be violated. Energy could be borrowed for short times, and, bizarrely, this energy could be used to make particles of matter like us, and other particles of a previously unknown type – known as antimatter. In nature it turns out that pairs of matter antimatter particles can pop into existence, live for a short time, and then recombine back into nothingness. Provided it all happens fast enough no one is any the wiser.

Private sector credit creation works like Heisenberg's matter antimatter pairs. Money and debt are created in pairs, from nothing, live for a while and then vanish when they recombine. Taking out a loan creates a money-debt pair, paying off the loan destroys a money-debt pair.

Recognising that private sector credit creation works through generating money and debt in combination is important in two respects. Firstly, it helps make it clear that private sector banking cannot be responsible for permanent ongoing inflation. Secondly, it helps clarify why some central banks worry so much about money supply growth; money growth also means debt growth, and it's the debt that causes financial instability.

Today there is a widespread misconception that private sector credit creation causes inflation. The truth is rather more subtle than this. As credit is being created – loans made – an inflationary impulse is generated, however when the credit is destroyed again – loans repaid – a deflationary impulse is generated. Provided loans are being made and destroyed at roughly equal rates the inflationary and deflationary impulses will tend to cancel, leaving prices stable. However, if either credit generation or credit destruction becomes dominant at any point, then respectively a temporary inflation or deflation will be generated. By extension, strong money supply growth today suggests inflation now and deflation in the future (be careful however as this is not yet the full picture). Financial instability can be generated if there are systems within the economy that tend to cause a predominance of credit creation in one period, followed by a predominance of credit destruction in the next.

Processes able to generate credit cycles are not part of the Efficient Market Hypothesis; however, one could imagine how they could arise if there were mechanisms within the financial markets which tended to cause a majority of agents within the economy to behave in the same way at the same time. The next chapters will discuss how such spontaneous self-ordering processes can be generated through positive feedback effects within the credit creation process.

The credit crisis and deflationary pressure of house prices today can therefore be thought of as a direct result of excessive credit creation in previous years. This is a pattern followed religiously by all asset boom-bust cycles.

Going back to the Great Depression of the 1930s the same story is apparent: strong credit growth in the 1920s with the development of hire purchase and instalment payments, followed by the credit contraction of the 1930s. Remarkably, however, today's accepted wisdom continues to blame the Great Depression solely on overly tight monetary policy in the 1930s, ignoring the contribution of excess credit generation in the 1920s.

3.3.9 Enter the central banks – as lender of last resort

Before we move onto the development of our modern fiat money system, now is a good time to start to think about how central banks fit into the picture. As previously explained, once the banking system started moving toward credit creation and fractional reserve banking, there was no longer enough gold in the system to honour all of the outstanding certificates of deposit. At least, that is, not without the banks first closing out all of their outstanding loans, which would require virtually an entire economic shutdown. In addition to which the depository receipt system established a network of interlocking obligations between the banks themselves that, as now, is highly problematic when the banks become concerned over each other's safety.

It soon became apparent, through repeated waves of financial crisis, that this new credit generation system was highly unstable. However, it was equally apparent that this new system was also leading to dramatic economic expansion, wealth generation and improving living standards. Going backward to a world before depository banks and credit creation was not an option. The process of credit creation had opened up a whole new channel for economic growth and prosperity. Venture capital in the truest sense of the word was now possible. Equally, the new banking system permitted channels by which risk could be pooled and shared; larger ventures became feasible. It was therefore clearly better to find a way to live with this new system rather than to live without it; a solution to the problem of bank runs was required.

The logical thing to do was to create a system to support troubled institutions, and another system of firewalls to prevent trouble at one bank spreading into a general panic throughout the entire system. The answer was a bank for banks – a central bank. The idea was that the central bank would, in the event of a crisis, take over the role of lending to a failing bank. If, as was sometimes the case, the bank was suffering a run due to a crisis of confidence but retained a basically sound loan book, then the central bank could support the institution until the panic faded and business could resume. If on the other hand the bank's loan book had turned bad, then the central bank would force the bank to close, while unwinding the loan book in an orderly manner.

For the central bank to be in a position to credibly prevent bank runs it must have and, more importantly must be thought to have, very large and preferably inexhaustible reserves. If the financial community believed the central bank to have virtually limitless resources, then once the bank announced that it was willing to defend any given institution, by honouring its obligations, the bank run would likely abate. In other words, if the community thought the central bank had enough gold reserves, the central bank would not need them.[31]

The role by which central banks lend to troubled private sector banks is referred to as "lender of last resort", so named because it was intended that turning to the central bank for finance should only be done once all other avenues for borrowing through the private sector were exhausted.

---

[31] It was this effect that the Bank of England hoped would prevent a bank run on Northern Rock. In theory, once it became public knowledge that the Bank of England was willing to lend to Northern Rock, the depositors should have considered their deposits safe and not withdrawn them. Unfortunately, this is not what happened. In practice, the depositors correctly viewed the bank's requirement to go to the Bank of England as a sign of weakness and, with the benefit of hindsight, the Bank of England's initial indication of support was perhaps too equivocal to prevent the run.

3.3.10 Financial crises happen with and without a gold standard

I have chosen to introduce the lender of last resort role, and the idea of central banks as a stabiliser of a fractional reserve gold-standard banking system at this stage of the story to make a number of related points. The original and still primary purpose of central banking is not, as is widely believed today, to fight inflation, rather it is to ensure financial stability of the credit creation system. Financial instability can occur in any credit-dominated system, with or without the gold standard. There are those who argue for a return to a gold standard currency; this move may cure certain problems, but it would not, as some argue, usher in a golden age of financial stability.

Those advocating the abolition of central banks in the hope of re-establishing financial stability would likely be disappointed. The question of which came first – financial instability or central banking – is not a chicken and egg question; history shows quite clearly that financial instability came before central banking. This point is well made by examining the events behind the 1907 crisis in America that occurred in the absence of a central bank. It was this crisis that demonstrated the necessity of the central bank and led directly to the formation of the US Federal Reserve System.[32] The American 1907 crisis helps answer the question of whether or not central banks are responsible for financial markets not behaving according to the predictions of the Efficient Market Hypothesis; the misbehaviour was already present before central banking emerged. Financial instability caused central banking, not the other way around (at least not originally).

---

[32] The history of the 1907 crisis is documented in "The Panic of 1907, Lessons Learned from the Market's Perfect Storm", by R. Bruner and S. Carr. This book tells the story of how a boom-bust credit cycle and the inability of the financial system to deal with a credit crisis required the legendary banker J.P. Morgan to adopt the role of central banker.

To re-establish financial stability would require not the reversion to a gold standard, or the abolition of the central banks; it would require nothing less than the abolition of credit creation. In other words we would need to return our economies to the dark ages. Credit creation must stay, and we must find a way to live with the instability that comes with it; it is better to have a volatile and growing economy than a stable and stagnant one.

3.3.11 Unintended consequences – enter the moral hazard

Having said that financial instability caused central banking, and not the other way round, I must quickly add caveats. The introduction of the lender-of-last-resort function had unfortunate adverse consequences. Firstly, the lender-of-last-resort provided the banks with another potential source of finance, which they could rely upon in the event of a crisis. Naturally this tended to make the banks more confident, and therefore willing to extend more loans. Secondly, because the lender-of-last-resort was seen as underwriting all banks equally, depositors and merchants were likely to treat them as being all equally reliable as one another. There was therefore no motivation for depositors to seek out the safest institutions in which to place their money, and no motivation for the merchants to differentiate between the quality of the banks' certificates of deposit.

The presence of the central bank therefore created a perverse incentive structure within the banking industry. Depositors would seek out the banks offering the highest rates of interest on their deposits paying no attention to the security of the bank – in the end all money would be repaid by the central bank. However, the banks that could afford to pay the highest rates of interest were likely to be those taking the most risk with depositors' money. The upshot was that the presence of a lender-of-last-resort created a rush of money toward the most risky institutions. This problem is one facet of the moral-hazard problem.[33]

An easy way to understand moral hazard is as follows: your child is off to university and you, being a good parent, would like to ensure that he or she does not run desperately short of money. So you give them a credit card, which draws directly on your bank account. As you hand over the card do you say:

A: Don't worry, the account's stuffed full of money; just use the card to pay off any overdraft you might happen to run up.

Or

B: Use the card only as a last resort; with all this damned inflation around we can barely afford to eat as it is.

Chances are you'll lean a little toward plan B, telling yourself it's good to teach some real-life money management skills.

The story is basically the same with the central banks and the banking system. In a crisis the central bank helps to stabilise the financial system, especially if the central bank is believed to have endlessly deep pockets. But between crises the presence of a central bank promotes more risky lending practices and therefore greater levels of debt – Friedman might just have a point.

Central banks were introduced to stabilise the credit system but then found that their presence encouraged more risky lending and inadvertently destabilised it.

---

[33] Arguably this was part of the problem behind the story of Northern Rock. The bank was able to attract funds with higher interest rates, which it was able to offer due to its more aggressive lending strategies. Investors were happy to take these higher rates without worrying about how their money was being used because it was considered impossible for a bank like Northern Rock to fail. As it turned out of course the depositors were correct; in the end their deposits were backed by the government. The Northern Rock story suggests the rational choice is to go for the highest rate of deposit interest available, regardless of the business model of the bank in question.

The presence of a central bank, willing to underwrite all deposits equally, will have the effect of putting safer, less leveraged, institutions at a commercial disadvantage relative to the more cavalier institutions. Over time this will lead to bad lending practices forcing out good lending practice. The introduction of a central bank created a race to the bottom, with all banks incentivised to take on more risk than their competitors.

Today most central banks prefer to downplay the lender-of-last-resort function precisely because advertising this function helps fuel dangerous lending practices. Unfortunately this point was not fully understood in the run-up to the current crisis when the US Federal Reserve began to actively communicate that they were adopting what was called a "risk management paradigm", designed to pre-empt economic weakness.[34]

The risk management paradigm effectively said: don't worry; we the lender-of-last-resort will come to your aid well before you reach the point of needing to borrow from us. In effect this policy gave carte blanche to use the credit card freely.

---

[34] See "Monetary Policy under Uncertainty" by Alan Greenspan, Jackson Hole, Wyoming August 29th, 2003:

'At times, policy practitioners operating under a risk-management paradigm may be led to undertake actions intended to provide some insurance against the emergence of especially adverse outcomes. For example, following the Russian debt default in the fall of 1998, the Federal Open Market Committee (FOMC) eased policy despite our perception that the economy was expanding at a satisfactory pace and that, even without a policy initiative, was likely to continue to do so. We eased policy because we were concerned about the low-probability risk that the default might severely disrupt domestic and international financial markets, with outsized adverse feedback to the performance of the U.S. economy.'

This passage explains how the US Federal Reserve moved toward a pre-emptive policy response to counteract anticipated economic weakness. As will be explained later, this minor move from re-active to pro-active policy turns a central bank from a mode of operation in which it attenuates crises to one in which it amplifies crises.

3.3.12 Central banks and centralized money

Once again the law of unintended consequences had kicked in; central banks, introduced to stabilize the system, became a source of destabilisation. And once again something had to be done. The answer was that the banks had to be controlled. In return for the backing of the central bank the commercial banks gave up the right to issue their own gold depository certificates. From now on there would be only one permitted type of depository certificate and these would be printed by the government, and be distributed through the central bank to the commercial banks. In addition, the gold reserves of the commercial banks would be collected together at the central bank.

Centralising the gold reserves had the beneficial effect of strengthening the position of the central bank, whose reserves of gold were now so large that it could deal with almost any size bank run. Equally significant was that the new arrangement allowed the central bank to control the commercial banks, who were no longer able to lend unchecked. The central bank would control the number of certificates in circulation and monitor the activities of each bank to ensure that no one bank was abusing the lender-of-last-resort facility.

The standardization to a single certificate of deposit also simplified the credit system tremendously. All certificates were now equally valuable, even in a crisis. This new system meant that it was possible to stabilise the banking system and to shackle the new problem of the moral hazard. All told the new arrangement was a tremendous leap forward.[35]

---

[35] One could imagine a congratulatory letter that may have been written to the then government minister responsible for engineering this new arrangement:

Dear Darling,

You have done such a wonderful job in bringing about this new monetary arrangement. The whole thing is so neat. Your old friends at the central bank must be delighted, being now able to check the rabble of bankers as a whole and to keep an eye on each individual troublemaker. Combining monetary management with banking supervision, under one roof – simply marvellous! Now the system really cannot be rocked – a masterstroke, pure genius! And don't you ever forget it, my Darling.

3.3.13 No need for any more mucking about with the smelter

This new monetary arrangement had an interesting side effect, which gives us an important clue on the trail of the Inflation Monster. Having taken hold of both the gold reserves for the whole monetary system and of the issuance of certificates of gold deposit (money), the central bank was now the only place where these certificates could be swapped back into gold. The government, through its control of the central bank, now had a monopoly on printing money (certificates of gold deposit) and on exchanging those certificates into real gold.

This new monopoly position of the government over the monetary system gave the state an important new power; the ability to change the amount of gold it was willing to pay out for each certificate in circulation.

As mentioned previously, under the old system of gold coinage governments occasionally conducted recoinage operations. This was essentially an exercise in confiscating its citizens' wealth: gold coins were recalled, melted down and reissued with a lower gold content. The leftover gold was used to make additional coins that went straight to the government.

As a tax-raising exercise this was a messy business. It was expensive and time-consuming to smelt the metal and re-stamp the coins, and it was also a little too obvious that the new coins were not as valuable as the old ones, making it difficult to prise the old gold coins from the grasping hands of the citizenry.

Under the new monetary regime the whole recoinage exercise was made much slicker. Now the government could simply adjust the amount of gold it was willing to pay out for each of the certificates (money) in circulation. There was no need to actually collect up and re-issue the money, just a short parliamentary decree announcing a new rate of conversion into gold.

For the government this was an excellent development. If, for example, the government had overspent and was having trouble extracting enough tax from its citizens, the government would simply announce a new gold conversion rate. In the morning your wad of notes could be convertible into one gold nugget, and in the evening only half a nugget – and you wouldn't even have to go to the bank to hand over the notes. This move then allowed the government to print itself some more money to pay off its debts. Of course the extra printed money meant that there was now more money chasing the same amount of goods and services so prices tended to rise, or, equivalently, the value of money tended to fall. This modern day recoinage exercise was known as devaluing the currency. All told, the movement to a centralized gold-standard paper-currency system made it much easier for a government to expropriate its citizens' wealth through devaluation.

While devaluations became easier from a practical point of view, they remained difficult from a political perspective; the government of the day still had the embarrassment of announcing the devaluation, which naturally was never popular with the rabble. In practice the political difficulty in adopting the devaluation policy imposed a significant degree of discipline on governments, and as a result devaluations were infrequent. Devaluation under a gold-standard paper-currency system brings us very close to the Inflation Monster, but we have not yet got to the point of the continuous inflation (devaluation) that is commonplace today.

Note that even now there is still no sign of any Inflation Monster throwing away money for free in the marketplace.

3.3.14 Closing in on the monster

The next step in the story is the movement from the gold standard to what is known as a "fiat" currency. This step occurred in different countries at different times, with some countries moving away from, and then back onto, a gold standard at different times. The most spectacular departure from the gold standard occurred in Germany in the 1920s when, in large part as a result of "The Economic Consequences Of The Peace"[36] treaty imposed on that country at the end of World War I, the German government attempted to shore up its finances by printing itself more money. For the purposes of this story, however, the next step will focus not on Germany's move to fiat currency but instead on America's.

3.3.15 Bretton Woods and the global gold standard

The story of America's migration from the gold standard to fiat money also begins with the two World Wars. As Keynes predicted, the consequences of the post-World War I peace treaty was disastrous. The treaty contributed to Germany's bankruptcy, hyperinflation and economic collapse. Having witnessed these events firsthand, the post-World War II agenda was quite different from that prevailing after World War I; reconstruction rather than retribution was the policy objective. A key element of this reconstruction policy was to ensure a stable global

---

[36] Once again John Maynard Keynes appears in the story. Following World War I, Keynes became part of the team responsible for imposing the peace settlement on the defeated Germany. Recognising that the proposed reparations demanded of Germany would bankrupt the country, Keynes resigned his position, and wrote "The Economic Consequences of the Peace", explaining the problem. Keynes was ignored, the treaty was imposed, and as predicted Germany was bankrupted. As part of the reparations process the German government was forced to pay away a large part of the gold reserves that backed its currency. These payments, coupled with the government resorting to printing still more currency, produced a spiralling hyperinflation. The resultant economic collapse is today recognised as being a significant element in the subsequent rise of extremism. In a nutshell – WWII was in part born from poor economic and monetary policy as a result of the treaty which ended WWI, and which Keynes opposed.

currency regime that would help all sides rebuild their economic infrastructure. The architecture of the post WWII currency system was decided upon at a conference in the American resort of Bretton Woods, just prior to the end of the war. The structure was simplicity itself: all major currencies would be valued against the US dollar at a fixed exchange rate. The value of the US dollar was in turn fixed at a price of $35 per ounce of gold. The combination of fixing all currencies against the dollar and all dollars against gold effectively put the whole world's currency system onto an agreed gold standard monetary system.[37]

3.3.16 Bretton Woods – edging toward the endgame

The Bretton Woods system worked very well for several decades helping facilitate the rapid reindustrialisation of both Europe and Japan.[38]

By the late 1960s, the reindustrialisation outside of America had been so successful that the trade position between America and the rest of the world had reversed; America was now buying more than it was selling. As a result the US was running a trade deficit with the rest of the world, which in turn meant that there was a net outflow of US dollars from America going to the rest of the world to pay for America's imports.

---

[37] Keynes had also been part of negotiating the Bretton Woods currency framework, and had recommended that all individual country currencies be pegged against a new global currency – the bancor. This new currency would then be managed by what would have been in effect a global central bank. Having seen the high price of ignoring Keynes's advice after WWI, the political establishment decided to also ignore his advice after WWII. Needless to say Keynes, as was his habit, was right once more as the Bretton Woods system did not prove durable.

[38] Technically the Bretton Woods framework was only part of the story. After the war America, with its relatively unscathed industrial base, was in trade surplus with the rest of the world whose own manufacturing base had been badly damaged. As a result goods were flowing out of America and dollars flowing back into America (to pay for the goods). This unbalanced flow produced an upward pressure on the US dollar versus other currencies, which was not permitted under the Bretton Woods framework. At the same time it drained dollars out of the reindustrialising countries, hampering their ability to import necessary goods from the US and therefore undermining the reconstruction effort. The solution to this problem was that America recycle the dollars back out to the rest of the world in the form of aid; the Marshall Aid Plan being a key conduit for this flow.

This unbalanced trade and currency flow tended to depress the value of the US dollar. However, under the Bretton Woods agreement non-US countries were obliged to keep the value of their currencies fixed with respect to the US dollar. To maintain these fixed exchange rates foreign governments were obliged to recycle the trade surplus back into America. Put differently, if the European currencies were to remain fixed with respect to the US dollar, then for every dollar America spent on European goods Europe would have to spend that same dollar amount on something in the US – that something was US government debt.[39]

---

[39] Under the terms of the Bretton Woods agreement non-US governments were obliged to maintain a fixed exchange rate for their currencies against the US dollar. This meant that once the US had fallen into a position of trade deficit with a foreign country, that country was compelled to purchase US dollars: Americans sent US dollars abroad to buy goods from foreign countries, and those foreign countries, through their governments, then had to send those dollars back, using the money to buy US government Treasuries.

Without the foreign governments returning the US dollars through purchasing Treasuries, the flow of currency out of America would have been mainly outward. That is to say there would have been more sellers of US dollars than buyers, which would have caused the US exchange rate to fall, in contravention of the Bretton Woods agreement.

Today the situation between the US and many of the key industrialising and commodity producing nations is much the same. The US is again funding a war through debt finance while running a major trade deficit with countries committed to a pegged (Middle East) or largely pegged (China and Asia) currency. These currency pegs can only be maintained with the recycling of the US trade deficit back into the US via debt purchases.

Both the US trade imbalances associated with the ending of the Bretton Woods agreements and those accumulated over recent years stand in testament to the fragility of fixed exchange rates. The underlying force behind both scenarios was a shifting of relative industrialisation and therefore trade flows. In the years after WWII Europe and Japan re-industrialised – they were the (re) emerging markets of their day – and as a result began exporting more goods to America. Had their currencies been free to float during this period the shifting trade pattern would have produced a progressive appreciation, helping maintain a more balanced trade pattern. In practice this arrangement allowed Europe and Japan to enjoy an artificial competitive advantage against America in the decades after WWII, thereby accelerating the rate of re-industrialisation in these regions. Generous as it was, this gift from America could not persist in perpetuity and was ended with the breakdown of the Bretton Woods system in 1971.

One of the consequences of today's fixed exchange rates is that foreign goods looked too cheap from a US perspective and no matter how much money America borrows from abroad that money is always recycled back into the American economy. As a result there is no mechanism to curtail US borrowing from abroad – foreign capital does not become more expensive no matter how much is borrowed.

While foreign governments continued accumulating ever-larger US dollar holdings the US government was, due to the Vietnam War, getting ever deeper into debt.

Paying for wars is an expensive business for governments. It can be done in one of three ways:

1. By raising taxes from its citizens

2. Through borrowing money

3. Through currency devaluation (the government prints itself more money)

Of course the second option – borrowing money – is only a method of delaying either the taxation or the devaluation. As the Vietnam War progressed, its popularity fell and its cost rose, making the taxation option politically inexpedient.

As the 1960s drew to a close it became obvious that the US government would have to resort to the printing press to pay off its debts. The foreign governments, who were holding so much US government debt, began to sense what was to come; America would have to devalue its currency, breaking the fixed exchange rate of $35 per ounce of gold.

3.3.17 Time to meet the monster

With foreign governments accumulating ever more US dollars in their reserves, and the US responding by printing more dollars as a replacement, economists began talking of a "Dollar Glut".[40] While the

---

[40] The economist Robert Triffin was foremost in demonstrating the unsustainable nature of the Bretton Woods framework. In 1966, Triffin wrote: 'The era of the "dollar gap" has been succeeded indeed by that of the "dollar glut".' (p65, "The World Money Maze"). Today, US policy makers prefer to cast the re-emergence of a "dollar glut" as an "Asian savings glut", neatly sending the problem of excessive domestic US credit creation abroad.

number of dollars was growing the stock of gold in the US reserves was not. The upshot of all of this was a bank run on an unprecedented scale. As it became obvious that the US government could no longer honour the convertibility of dollars into gold some of the more informed of the foreign governments, who were holding US dollars, decided to tender their holdings for conversion into gold.

US President Richard Nixon knew that this request for the conversion of foreign reserves into gold could spiral into a bank run in the form of an avalanche of conversion requests, which in the end he could not honour. Nixon was faced with a choice of paying away the American gold reserves to honour the first requests, and then defaulting on the later requests, or simply refusing all requests for conversion. Nixon made the rational choice; he kept the gold and went directly for currency devaluation. On August 15th 1971, Nixon announced the closure of the gold window; the US dollar ceased to be a certificate of gold deposit currency. And, as the Bretton Woods agreement pegged all other currencies to gold via the dollar, the rest of the world was also taken off the gold standard.

The closure of the US gold window and the end of US dollar convertibility into gold ushered in an entirely new monetary regime. Previous devaluations had generally involved setting a new lower exchange rate between the currency and gold, but under the post-1971 arrangement the convertibility of money into gold was dispensed with entirely.

For Nixon this was a masterstroke, as it allowed the US dollar denominated debt to be funded simply by printing more dollars. And without a gold peg there was no longer any need for the embarrassing procedure of having the government announce a currency devaluation. Instead, a rolling undeclared devaluation could be implemented. Our modern monetary regime had come into being, and with it the Inflation Monster had been born. Governments were now free to print money at will.

3.3.18 Money, anti-money and fiat money

The new currency regime, without a gold exchange rate, is known as fiat money. The movement from a currency backed by gold to one with no fixed gold price represented a momentous shift in our financial architecture.

The invention of gold depository banks and thereafter the development of fractional reserve banking created the first type of credit creation process. The banks were able to create money, from thin air, by literally printing and handing out certificates of deposit. But for each certificate of deposit that was handed out the banks also created a corresponding debt (money – anti-money). The advent of fiat money allowed for an entirely new mechanism of monetary creation. Governments had now awarded themselves the right to create their own money without any corresponding liability; since there was no longer a promise to convert the printed money into gold, there was no longer a liability associated with printing that money.

We have now identified the modern Inflation Monster, a beast that can conjure money from thin air and give it away for nothing. We could even give the monster a birthday and a surname, if we felt so inclined. But even this monster is still not the beast described in the ECB's cartoon. This monster does not roam the streets distributing money to the hoi polloi; rather it is kept caged, deep in the bowels of the state, and used exclusively to print money for the government.

This brings us to one of central banking's dirty little secrets. The Inflation Monster is part of government, and central banking is also part of government. The central banks and the Inflation Monster are not quite one in the same entity but they are very close cousins.

3.3.19 From printing press to price spiral

For a while it appeared that Nixon's abandonment of the gold peg, and the subsequent breakdown of fixed exchange rates, had given governments a fountain of free wealth. Some governments took to this new regime like a duck to water; the British government proved themselves particularly adept with the press. The Germans, who had seen the movie before, knew it quickly moved from farce to tragedy, and chose to refrain from the temptations of the press. To cut a long story short, some governments printed more and more money, and used this to increase their spending. The extra government spending pushed up prices, and reduced the spending power of people's wages. Workers demanded higher wages, companies provided these higher wages by putting up their prices. These higher prices in turn reduced the spending power of the government, who responded by printing itself still more money.

After a few years of this inflation spiral it became apparent that the ever-shifting prices were damaging the performance of the economy. Businesses could not reliably forecast costs, or revenues, and therefore cut back on investment; economies stalled, while inflation continued unchecked – stagflation was born.

The movement from a gold standard currency to a fiat money system had changed the laws of economics; it was now possible to get low economic activity and high inflation at the same time.

3.3.20 A little less brandy m'lord

The invention of fiat money had given governments the keys to the monetary drinks cabinet, allowing them to binge on the wealth of their citizens. However, the economic damage caused by the resulting price spiral could not be tolerated indefinitely.

The solution to the inflation problem came about in two ways. Firstly, governments began to accept that they should, and would have to, balance their budgets, bringing expenditure into line with their tax revenue. Secondly, the central banks were given the new responsibility of controlling inflation. The deal was basically as follows: if the government started generating inflation by printing money, the central bank would respond by raising interest rates. This would have the effect of making it more expensive for private sector companies and households to borrow money. The commercial banks would therefore reduce their lending – an increase in printed money was to be offset by decreasing private sector credit creation. This arrangement provided a reasonable discipline on the government, who now knew that an attempt to increase their revenue through the printing press would be futile as it would lead the central banks to trigger a recession by hiking rates, which would then reduce the government's revenue.

It may be useful to think of this new arrangement between governments and central banks as something akin to that between a habitually drunken lord and his trusty manservant. In a moment of hung-over sobriety, the lord hands the keys to the drinks cabinet to his manservant, instructing him to ration his future drinking. The manservant now has the unenviable role of being both in control of his master and in the employ of his master. To perform this task the manservant must be sufficiently secure in his tenure to stand up to his boss's demands for liquor – the servant must have independence. Similarly, central bankers must have sufficient power and independence from government to discipline governments and to resist their attempts to print excessive amounts of money. It is for this reason that a central bank must remain outside of political control.

In today's modern political framework this necessity for central bank independence poses the delicate problem of requiring an institution that is, to some degree, above democratic control. Having such an important institution unaccountable to democratic process makes it all the more important that its remit and operating parameters be well and widely understood.

3.3.21 An error of omission or commission

The introduction of fiat money gave birth to the Inflation Monster, changed the way our monetary system worked and revolutionised the role of the central bank. In the same educational section of the ECB's website which hosts the Inflation Monster movie there is also a 90-page booklet of materials for teachers on the topic of money. Part of this document contains a history of money. Like my own history, the story progresses from barter to gold, then to gold coins and paper money. But when it comes to telling the story of fiat money the history is cut short; all that is offered is:

> The Bretton Woods system collapsed in 1971, and since then the currencies of the major economies have remained pure fiat money.

No further explanation of fiat money is offered. Given the significance of fiat money in the inflation process it is unfortunate that fiat money is not better explained and more widely understood.

In what was, for a senior central banker, a rare moment of candour, the now-US Fed Chairman, Ben Bernanke explained the connection between fiat money and inflation with somewhat more clarity:

> A little parable may prove useful: Today an ounce of gold sells for $300, more or less. Now suppose that a modern alchemist solves his subject's oldest problem by finding a way to produce unlimited amounts of new gold at essentially no cost. Moreover, his invention

is widely publicized and scientifically verified, and he announces his intention to begin massive production of gold within days. What would happen to the price of gold? Presumably, the potentially unlimited supply of cheap gold would cause the market price of gold to plummet. Indeed, if the market for gold is to any degree efficient, the price of gold would collapse immediately after the announcement of the invention, before the alchemist had produced and marketed a single ounce of yellow metal.

What has this got to do with monetary policy? Like gold, U.S. dollars have value only to the extent that they are strictly limited in supply. But the U.S. government has a technology, called a printing press (or, today, its electronic equivalent), that allows it to produce as many U.S. dollars as it wishes at essentially no cost. By increasing the number of U.S. dollars in circulation, or even by credibly threatening to do so, the U.S. government can also reduce the value of a dollar in terms of goods and services, which is equivalent to raising the prices in dollars of those goods and services. We conclude that, under a paper-money system, a determined government can always generate higher spending and hence positive inflation.

Of course, the U.S. government is not going to print money and distribute it willy-nilly...[41]

Those remarks were made at the end of 2002. Now, several deficit spending years later, gold sells for closer to $1,000 an ounce. The connections between inflation and deficit spending remain very much in place.

It is important to recognise that this new fiat money system has only been in operation since 1971. What's more, the inflationary problems

---

[41] "Deflation: Making Sure "It" Doesn't Happen Here", remarks by Governor Ben S. Bernanke, before the National Economists Club, Washington, DC, November 21st, 2002.

associated with the abandonment of the gold peg were not immediately appreciated and as a consequence central banks have had less than four decades experience of how best to adapt to their new task of inflation policeman, and to learn how that task interacts with their still existing role of ensuring the stability of the private sector fractional reserve banking system.

3.3.22 A brief aside – on the topic of inflation and taxation

Today the central banks all have very similar, stated or unstated, inflation objectives which tend to cluster around a level of a 2% annual increase in the price of goods and services. There are a number of good reasons for having this target as a positive number rather than at perfect price stability of zero per cent year-on-year inflation.

One reason for a positive inflation target is an effect known as nominal price rigidity, meaning people don't like cutting prices, especially if those prices happen to be their wages. Nevertheless, some jobs do get less valuable over time and should see their wage rates fall relative to those of other industries. In practice it is just easier to cut wages in real terms, by allowing average wages to drift up while holding some wages constant, than it is to tell someone that they must take a pay cut. Another reason for seeking a positive average inflation rate is because this means that interest rates are generally higher on average, which makes it easier for the central bank to manage credit cycles; if interest rates are higher, then a central bank has more room to cut them when it decides it needs to stimulate the economic activity by encouraging more borrowing.[42] The third reason for a positive inflation target is

---

[42] When lending money, investors require compensation for any lost purchasing power, caused by inflation, over the period of the loan. If you lend money for a year, and prices are rising by 5% per year, at the end of the loan you want your money back plus 5% to take account of the lost purchasing power, plus a little more to compensate you for your trouble (credit risk, lost opportunities, etc). As a result professional investors talk of an interest rate being composed of two parts – the inflation rate and the real rate. The real rate is what you really earn after accounting for losses due to inflation.

that, as mentioned, it provides a rather convenient tax, which, for the most part, people do not object to – as Jean-Baptiste Colbert said:

> *The art of taxation consists in so plucking the goose as to obtain the maximum amount of feathers with the smallest possible amount of hissing.*

The modern taxation system is tremendously efficient. First you're taxed when you earn money (income tax) and then again when you spend it (value added or consumption tax). But between what you earn, after tax, and what you spend there is occasionally a little bit left over, which we call savings, and without inflation governments can find it very difficult to help themselves to this bit in the middle. However, with inflation, a whole realm of taxes on savings becomes viable. Ensuring a positive inflation rate increases asset prices, and these price rises can be converted into capital gains and estate tax receipts. Even more importantly, higher inflation boosts interest rates and governments can then tax interest income. Consider the following examples:

Inflation is 0% per year and the real interest rate is 2% per year. So you earn a grand total of:

0%+2% = 2% interest

Of this the government takes a modest 40%, so all told you earn 1.2% interest per year, after tax. Not great but at least it's positive.

Now let's say inflation is 2% and the real interest rate is still 2%. Now you're earning 4% on your savings. The government takes 40% of that, leaving you with an after-tax interest rate of 2.4% per year. This is much better: you're earning twice as much.

Go one step further, to an inflation rate of 4% and a real interest rate still at 2%. Now your pre-tax interest is 6% and your after-tax rate is 3.6% – even better. From the government's perspective the tax take has gone from 0.8%, to 1.6% to finally 2.4% per year. Everyone wins!

Everyone wins, that is, until you start to think about your after-tax after-inflation adjusted interest rate. This has fallen from 1.2% in the first example to 0.4% in the second and to -0.4% in the third.

Between the scissors of tax and inflation even very modest inflation rates can achieve the effect of turning over all, or more than all, the real interest earned on savings to the government.[43]

The ability to print unlimited currency gives the government the ability to repay *any* amount of debt;[44] the government may choose to repay its own debt, or if it so chooses, private sector debt. However, engineering debt repayment through the printing press is not a free lunch, as it produces permanent irreversible inflation. If the government uses this facility to repay its own debt, then the inflation has effectively generated a net transfer of spending power, and wealth, from the private to the state sector; it should therefore be seen as a form of tax. However, if the government uses the printed money to repay or subsidise private sector

---

[43] Recall that the higher inflation comes from the government having printed themselves more money in the first place.

[44] The ability to repay debt through the printing press is confined to debt denominated in the country's own currency. An attempt to use the printing press to repay foreign denominated debt would result in a collapse in the foreign exchange value of the currency being printed, ending in a requirement to print even more currency.

debt, the effect is to redistribute wealth and purchasing power within the private sector.[45]

If one accepts that taxation is necessary, then there is nothing inherently wrong with using the inflation mechanism to generate tax income, though it would be healthier if the mechanism were more widely understood.

Another side effect of fiat money is that, through the printing press, central banks now have access to unlimited reserves and therefore it is entirely impossible to exhaust the central bank's reserves (in its own currency). Equally, it is impossible to bankrupt a government, provided it has borrowed only in its own currency. The move from the gold standard to fiat money made government finances and the central banks unbreakable. This unbreakable quality has its uses, especially in times of crises, but it also removes a key, perhaps the key, financial discipline.

We shall leave the story of inflation and taxation in the more capable hands of none other than Keynes himself:

> *Lenin is said to have declared that the best way to destroy the Capitalist System was to debauch the currency. By a continuing process of inflation, governments can confiscate, secretly and unobserved, an important part of the wealth of their citizens. By this method they not only confiscate, but they confiscate arbitrarily; and, while the process impoverishes many, it actually enriches some. The sight of this arbitrary rearrangement of riches*

---

[45] Dealing with the overhang of private sector mortgage debt in the US will quite likely result in an inflationary wealth redistribution. A government subsidy of private sector mortgage debt could result in an increased government debt, which is later monetized away through the printing press. Those that had saved, and therefore been able to lend money would see the purchasing power of their savings eroded, while those that had borrowed money would see the real cost of their debt also eroded. The upshot of all of this would be a net transfer of wealth from the prudent to the reckless – hence the term 'moral hazard'.

strikes not only at security, but at confidence in the equity of the existing distribution of wealth. Those to whom the system brings windfalls, beyond their desserts and even beyond their expectations or desires, become 'profiteers,' who are the object of the hatred of the bourgeoisie, whom the inflation has impoverished, not less than of the proletariat. As the inflation proceeds and the real value of the currency fluctuates wildly from month to month, all permanent relations between debtors and creditors, which form the ultimate foundation of capitalism, become so utterly disordered as to be almost meaningless; and the process of wealth-getting degenerates into a gamble and a lottery.

Lenin was certainly right. There is no subtler, no surer means of overturning the existing basis of society than to debauch the currency. The process engages all the hidden forces of economic law on the side of destruction, and does it in a manner which not one man in a million is able to diagnose.[46]

3.4 Yet another demand – demand management

So far we have discussed the central bank's jobs of underwriting the credit markets, as lender-of-last resort, and of controlling inflation as policeman of the printing press; to complete the modern central banker's job specification we must now discuss the role of demand management. In a nutshell, demand management means conducting fiscal and monetary policy in such a way as to dampen or eliminate the effect of economic recessions. In practice this means that when

---

[46] "The Economic Consequences of the Peace", J. M. Keynes, 1919, Chapter 6 'Europe After The Treaty.

economic growth slows, to a level considered unacceptable, governments are expected to boost activity through fiscal measures – tax cuts and public spending – while central banks are expected to cut interest rates to encourage more spending through more borrowing.

The task of demand management has now become part of what all central bankers are expected to do, and to varying degrees a role that central bankers have accepted. In the US, the Federal Reserve, under the leadership of Alan Greenspan, appeared to take to the role of demand manager with some enthusiasm, while in Europe the central bankers at the ECB came across as much more reticent.

To understand what modern demand management is, and how it evolved, we have to go back once more the writings of Mr Keynes and to the great depression. The Roaring Twenties in America was a period of remarkable economic progress: automobiles, radios, early household appliances and agricultural machinery were being developed and marketed. These new goods were useful and had a long life, but to many people the high upfront price was an insurmountable obstacle to their purchase. The solution to this problem came in the form of hire-purchase arrangements and instalment payments – consumer credit was born.

The expansion of consumer credit made the new consumer durables affordable to a mass market and spurred the enormous economic expansion of the roaring 1920s. Booming industry naturally translated into a booming stock market. As is well known, this boom came to an abrupt end with the stock market crash of October 1929, and thereafter the US economy fell into the seemingly inescapable Great Depression of 1930s.

Two economists came forward to explain the depression: Irving Fisher in America and Keynes in England. Fisher published his theory "The debt-deflation theory of great depressions" in 1933, arguing that the depression was caused due to an overhang of debt accumulated in the boom of the 1920s. His theory suggested that once an economy began to contract, the real burden of the previously accumulated debt began to grow, which in turn generated a further depressing force on the economy. In his 1935 book "The General Theory of Employment Interest and Money", Keynes went a step further than Fisher, presenting a theory that explained both how a depression was formed and more usefully how it could be reversed. In the early 1930s the reputation of Fisher was unfortunately damaged by him having been one of the primary cheerleaders of the stock market bubble; just prior to the crash he famously declared 'stock prices have reached what looks like a permanently high plateau'. By contrast, the reputation of Keynes was riding high, not least because his principled stance against the World War I peace treaty had unfortunately been vindicated by the subsequent economic collapse of Germany. Keynes' stronger reputation, coupled with the fact that he offered a strategy to end the Great Depression, meant that the recommendations of his "General Theory" quickly gained traction.

Keynes' "General Theory" was a radical departure from what he called classical economics. He explained in the preface to his book that he was attacking not just the detail of classical economic theory but rather its core premises:

> For if economics is at fault, the error is to be found not in the superstructure, which has been erected with great care for logical consistency, but in a lack of clearness and of generality in the premises.

The basic premise of economic theory that Keynes was attacking was none other than the idea of efficient markets. His "General Theory" presented a detailed description of mechanisms by which economies can become stuck in situations of depressed economic activity, far removed from the optimal equilibrium forecast by the theories of market efficiency. The Keynesian breakthrough was that he then explained how to escape these traps through deficit spending.

The key to Keynes' policy recommendation was that when an economy became trapped in a protracted depression, the government should increase its spending, without increasing taxation, thereby engaging in deficit spending. This was a radical departure from previous thinking, where the received wisdom was that in depressed economic circumstances it was prudent to reduce, not increase, government expenditure.

Not only did Keynes tell governments that they should spend more, he even told them that to spend recklessly was better than not to spend at all. The following passage, from the "General Theory", gives a flavour of the policy action that Keynes claimed could combat recession:

If the Treasury were to fill old bottles with bank-notes, bury them at suitable depths in disused coal-mines which are then filled up to the surface with town rubbish, and then leave it to private enterprise on well-tried principles of laissez-faire to dig the notes up again (the right to do so being obtained, of course, by tendering for leases of the note-bearing territory), there need be no more unemployment and, with the help of the repercussions, the real income of the community, and its capital wealth also, would probably become a good deal greater than it actually is.

Keynes was not actually recommending that government spend money in such bizarre wasteful ways. His real message was that deficit spending should be used for productive tasks, but that it was the spending and not the task itself that would help push an economy out of a depression. A respected economist recommending foolish government spending – needless to say the idea was an instant hit with the political class, and has remained in vogue ever since. Keynesian spending policies were tried in the 1930s and found to work; once again Keynes was vindicated.

3.4.1 Bastardising the insight of Keynes

In the period of a little more than seventy years since Keynes wrote his "General Theory", his policy recommendations and his theoretical insight have undertaken two quite remarkably divergent journeys: Keynes' repudiation of market efficiency has been almost entirely ignored; while his policy of fiscal stimulus, derived from that repudiation, has been accepted wholeheartedly and applied with a degree of enthusiasm which almost certainly far exceeded his original intention.

Keynesian policy is now enacted through two channels. Governments use fiscal stimulus to boost economic activity by spending more than their tax revenue. And central banks use monetary policy to encourage the private sector to borrow, thereby boosting consumption and investment relative to income. Both government deficit spending and the lowering of the private sector savings rate have the effect of boosting spending and therefore demand in the economy.

It is important to recognise that both fiscal and monetary stimulus policies work in the same way by spurring debt-fuelled spending.

Where modern stimulus policy differs substantially from Keynes' original recommendations is in the timing of how these policies are deployed. Keynes was writing in the 1930s at the depths of the Great Depression, and was therefore advising the implementation of stimulus policies as a way of getting out of a depression, that is from a point of already depressed activity. Today Keynesian stimulus is used not to exit depressions but rather to avoid going into recessions. The difference between these two applications of Keynesian policy is subtle, but forms an important part of the financial instability story and the story of today's credit crunch.

As originally advised, Keynesian policy requires stimulating an economy once it has already suffered an economic recession, when the overall level of economic activity has already contracted significantly. Today we deploy Keynesian stimulus not when activity has already fallen, but instead when the rate of growth of the economy is slowing, or expected to slow. The first flavour of Keynesianism means policy is reactive, coming after the credit contraction; the second flavour means that policy is proactive, and is applied to prevent the credit contraction. If successful, this proactive version of Keynesian policy can avoid a recession altogether, or at least make it much shallower and less painful than it would otherwise have been.

However, the successes of pre-emptive Keynesianism means that borrowers are denied the opportunity to learn that their excessive borrowing was indeed excessive. As each fledgling recession is successfully prevented by the government and the central bank, the private sector borrowers become progressively more confident and therefore willing to build up an even greater stock of debt. However, as the debt stock builds it becomes progressively more difficult for the stimulus policies to offset future downturns.

Government and central bank stimulus policies applied after borrowers have experienced the cathartic lesson of a recession is a sustainable strategy, but pre-emptive stimulus is ultimately not sustainable.

3.4.2 The efficient markets and Keynesian stimulus

It is worth taking the time to consider just how deep a conflict there is between Keynesian stimulus policies and the principles of efficient markets. From the monetary policy aspect, the central bank reduces interest rates as the economy slows. This policy is designed to manage the demand for credit (encourage more of it) and to fight the private capital market's natural tendency to raise interest rates at times of crisis, neither of which should be necessary in an efficient self-optimising market.[47]

When one realises that fiscal stimulus is a procedure whereby governments borrow and spend money on behalf of their citizens, because the governments judge that their citizens are saving too much of their own money, the full conflict with the principles of free and efficient markets becomes clear.

3.4.3 Who are the Keynesians?

Given the extent of the conflict between Keynesian policy and efficient market philosophy, it would be natural to expect demand management to be unpopular amongst the supporters of the Efficient Market Hypothesis. Interestingly this is not how things have evolved. Today the manipulation of interest rates for the purpose of demand management is practiced most avidly in the US by the Federal Reserve, where arguably the commitment to the idea of market efficiency is

---

[47] Typically in an economic downturn the banks become more concerned over rising defaults leading them to demand higher interest rates to compensate for the higher risks. Occasionally the banks will choose to ration credit, refusing to lend to some borrowers on any terms. This cycle has been very much evident in the recent housing market bubble where credit conditions were eased in the economic expansion – when easier credit was not needed – and are now being tightened in the contraction – when easier credit is needed. This process alone is sufficient to undermine the Efficient Market Hypothesis.

strongest. Both the Federal Reserve's willingness to cut interest rates aggressively, and the size of the US government's recent fiscal stimulus packages stand in testament to their wholehearted embrace of Keynesian policy.

At first sight it is difficult to comprehend how the Keynesian manipulation of markets has been assimilated into the free market consensus without that consensus then collapsing under the weight of internal contradiction.

The contorted logic used to meld stimulus policies with efficient market principles appears to run something along the following lines. Markets are efficient, therefore the natural equilibrium state is one of maximum possible economic output. It follows, therefore, that any decrease in economic output must be a move away from equilibrium. And from this observation it follows that any and all economic contractions are not free market processes and should therefore be counteracted by stimulus policies. Efficient market economies should never contract unless subjected to an adverse external shocks, and these shocks should be counteracted with stimulus policies.[48] The unmentioned inconsistency in this argument is of course: efficient markets should be self-optimising, and therefore should be able to adapt to external shocks without the help of stimulus policies.

---

[48] As a rule an economist believing in market efficiency will seek to explain economic contractions with recourse to external (exogenous) events, whereas one more sceptical of market efficiency will be willing to entertain the idea that cycles can be generated by forces internal to the economy (endogenous). In future years the free market school will likely present the current credit crisis as arising through external shocks – oil will quite likely be put in the frame – whereas the free market sceptics will view the crisis as internally generated, by excess credit created during the housing bubble.

In short, today's efficient market consensus has adopted Keynesian stimulus policy, dramatically extended its implementation and at the same time forgot that these policies were born out of a sophisticated repudiation of efficient market theory. Needless to say, the intellectual bankruptcy of this position does not make for good policy.

3.5 Central banks – in today's credit crisis

The lender-of-last-resort function is today plain to see both in America, with the events surrounding the Bear Stearns story, and in the UK with Northern Rock. In both cases these banks suffered bank runs, becoming pariahs in the private capital markets, and were therefore forced to turn to their respective central banks for funds. Aware of the complex interlocking nature of the credit agreements between these and other firms, and the potentially devastating effect on confidence in other institutions, both the Fed and the Bank of England stepped in to support the two banks.

Quite early in the financial crisis the US Federal reserve began cutting interest rates aggressively. The object of this exercise was to persuade households, and especially house buyers, to continue borrowing and spending freely, and to counteract the adverse effect of higher interest rates caused by credit concerns. In the UK and Europe, however, the central banks have shown themselves to be much more reluctant to engage in early-stage demand management through lower interest rates.

3.6 Conflicted objectives

When thinking about the central bank's role of demand manager, and their role as guardian of financial stability, it is important to appreciate how this interacts with the price stability objective. Supporting demand through interest rate policy means one thing and one thing only: lowering interest charges to encourage more borrowing. However, as explained by the discussion of fractional reserve banking, more borrowing increases bank leverage, which in turn causes the type of financial fragility leading up to events like those of the Bear Stearns and Northern Rock stories. Financial stability therefore requires limiting credit expansion while demand management requires maintaining credit expansion – the two roles do not sit well together, especially if the central bank is of a mindset to prevent any and all credit contractions.

The Efficient Market Hypothesis dismisses the idea that an economy can generate an excessive level of credit creation, and views any economic expansion as a sign of an economy moving toward the hypothesised stable equilibrium. As a result, the central bank tends to ignore the role of monitoring and managing credit expansion and focuses instead on the demand management role.

Over time the successful implementation of demand management means that the economy goes through successive waves of credit expansions. However, as the stock of debt rises the central bank eventually reaches a point whereby lowering interest rates is not sufficient to encourage more private sector borrowing; private sector lenders refuse to pass on the central banks lower interest rates, and anyway, borrowers become concerned over their ability to pay off their stock of debt as well as their ability to meet interest payments. Once this point is reached the central bank is left with an ineffective monetary policy, and a highly indebted economy. This then brings about the conflict with the central bank's other job of guardian of the printing press.

Allowing an economy to free fall into recession from a point of extreme over indebtedness is extremely dangerous, risking a self-reinforcing economic collapse along the lines of that which happened in the Great Depression. The alternative is to simply pay off the debt through the printing press. Quite simply the government prints itself more money. It may then spend that money to generate inflation, to make the debt less burdensome, and it may even give some of the printed money to those that are indebted. But of course this inflationary "get out of jail card" requires the central bank to discard its new role of guardian of price stability.

3.7 Central banking – the story so far

We have a fiat money banking system with two distinct flavours of money creation: private sector credit creation (money created together with debt) and the public sector printing press (money created from thin air without offsetting debt). The former creates financial instability and inflation-deflation cycles; the latter creates one-way irreversible positive inflation.

Central banking was born out of a need to manage the innate instability of the fractional reserve banking system through the provision of a lender-of-last-resort. The moral hazard problem, created by the lender-of-last-resort, then required a subsequent monitoring and management of credit creation within the banking system. But the Efficient Market Hypothesis taught (some) central banks to disregard the need for credit management. Central banks were then given the job of maintaining price stability by preventing governments from printing too much money. Finally the central banks adopted, or had foisted upon them, the additional role of demand management, requiring them to ensure economic recessions were avoided.

The upshot of all this is that central banks are required to:

- Restrain credit creation for financial stability

- Promote credit creation for demand management

- Restrain monetization to control inflation

- Promote monetization to avoid economic contractions, after, that is, their policies of promoting credit expansion have been too successful

Some central banks think they should not accept the role of restraining credit creation, while others believe they should resist the role of demand management. Those that believe in efficient markets also believe in manipulating markets; using policies devised by a man who explained markets were not efficient.

Remarkably, this dog's dinner of conflicting objectives, incoherent theories, and confused policies, represents the current state of the art of central banking. Unremarkably, we find ourselves caught in a succession of financial crises as a result.

3.8 Where now?

This chapter has introduced money, central banking, inflation and some aspects of financial instability, while at the same time conveying some of the disarray and confusion surrounding macroeconomic policy and central banking today. The current global credit crisis argues that we can no longer afford to ignore the failings of monetary policy and our broader macroeconomic management strategy. But before we can get to a more coherent framework for monetary and macroeconomic policy we must first dispense with the Efficient Market Hypothesis once and for all.[49]

---

[49] Before leaving this chapter, the topic of Japan and the persistence of Japanese deflation must be addressed. Having claimed that governments can generate inflation at will by printing money, the persistence of Japanese deflation must be explained. Does the Japanese experience repudiate the idea that governments can always generate inflation?

Japan's inflation-generating capacity has been constrained by two factors. Most importantly, Japan has enjoyed a considerable trade surplus throughout its period of deflation. Any attempt to generate inflation through monetization (printing money) would have caused the value of the yen to fall sharply. This in turn would have caused an already large trade surplus to grow still larger, something that would have been intolerable to Japan's trade partners. Secondly, Japan's political/demographic structure places the balance of power in the older generation who have significant pension assets, largely invested in bonds. For this cohort, mild deflation is a perfectly acceptable state of affairs, again suggesting political factors put limits on the degree to which the printing press could be deployed.

Were the political climate to change, Japan could create inflation instantaneously. A simple decree allowing the holder of every bank note to add an extra zero to the number in the corners of the notes, and another decree requiring shopkeepers to accept the notes at their new higher denomination, would be enough to get shopkeepers marking up prices immediately. (I hasten to add: this is a thought experiment not a policy recommendation.)

4

Stable And Unstable Markets

'Every individual necessarily labours to render the annual revenue of society as great as he can. He generally indeed neither intends to promote the public interest, nor knows how much he is promoting it...He intends only his own gain, and he is in this, as in many other cases, led by an invisible hand to promote an end which was no part of his intention...By pursuing his own self-interest he frequently promotes that of society more effectually than when he really intends to promote it. I have never known much good done by those who affected to trade for the public good.'

Adam Smith, An Inquiry into the Nature and Causes of the Wealth of Nations, I,IV,2

4.1 Self-Interest Becomes Efficient Markets

The above quote is one of Adam Smith's three references to his famous *invisible hand*. It is clear from the context of Smith's passage that the term 'invisible hand' is here being used to refer to the benefit of encouraging the pursuit of self-interest; today, however, the term is widely used to describe the idea that markets have an inherently self-optimizing, self-stabilising quality. Central to this philosophy is that markets must be adaptive and stable. Put differently, for markets to be efficient stable systems they must, when disturbed, be able to reorganize themselves in response to the disturbance, and be able to find the new configuration of market prices that correspond to a new optimal allocation of resources, in the new equilibrium state. What absolutely cannot happen in an efficient market is for the effect of a small initial disturbance to become amplified without limit by forces generated by processes internal to the market. The thesis of this chapter is that the presence of market stability has been plausibly argued for the markets of goods and services, but that these arguments do not hold for asset markets, credit markets and the capital market system in general. It will be argued that once disturbed asset and credit markets are prone to undergo expansions and contractions that, in principle, have no limit and no stable equilibrium state.

To understand the fundamental difference in behaviour between the markets for goods and those for assets consider a hypothetical market square:

- Mondays, Wednesdays and Fridays the market sells goods and services

- Tuesdays, Thursdays and Saturdays the market sells assets and makes loans

To keep things simple, the goods market sells only bread and potatoes (there must always be at least one baker in these stories), and the asset market sells only stocks and makes loans.

4.2 It's Monday And It's Market Day – For Goods

As with any traditional town market the merchants arrive early in the morning, setting out their stalls, and displaying both the goods for sale and the prices at which they are offered. The baker's stall is laden with freshly baked bread, in front of which is a board showing the prices of his wares. On this particular Monday the baker has no reason to believe that the day's trading conditions will be any different from those of last week, so the prices he shows are the same as those with which he closed business on the previous Friday.

The farmer goes through the same routine, piling his stall high with potatoes and marking up his board with today's prices. The farmer, who has been harvesting his potatoes over the weekend, has been pleasantly surprised by the size of his crop. Knowing that he needs to sell more potatoes than usual today, he begins the day's trading with prices just a little lower than those of last Friday.

With the stalls set-up and the prices on display, the first customers begin to arrive. The customers survey the offerings and begin their purchases. Potatoes appear a little better value today and one or two customers revise their shopping lists accordingly. As the farmer intended, his slightly lower prices generate a little extra demand to meet his larger supply of potatoes.

The baker, on the other side of the square, who has no idea of the potato glut, notices his bread is selling a little more slowly than usual. He lowers his prices accordingly, and shortly thereafter finds business recovering.

A little later the farmer, unaware of the baker's now cheaper bread, notices the initial potato rush has faded slightly; he too edges his prices lower. Unknown to one another, the baker and farmer continue their price war, each ratcheting down their prices in turn. As the baker and farmer cut their prices, the shoppers begin to notice that *both* bread and potatoes are unusually cheap today; they in turn decide to buy just a little more than originally intended.

Toward the end of the day both the baker and farmer are selling their goods at a rate that they are happy with; prices have settled to a new stable equilibrium. The price of potatoes and bread have moved relative to one another, accommodating the extra supply of potatoes, and the average price of all goods has moved, reflecting the general shift in their supply. The price mechanism has generated extra demand just where needed, the equilibrium of supply and demand has been preserved, and the two stallholders never once communicated. Supply and demand is maintained by competitive market forces, with no requirement for external management.

Later in the day the market is shocked; from out of the West comes a lone rider on a mission to buy bread. Once again the price dance begins. The new demand for bread allows the baker to put up his prices. Shoppers turn away from bread and back to potatoes. The farmer is also able to raise prices. After a few adjustments a new market equilibrium is established. Initially the townsfolk are upset at the stranger for pushing up prices, but as he becomes a regular feature of the marketplace the baker responds by baking some extra loaves each day, and the prices fall back down. Extra demand creates extra supply; again via the price mechanism, equilibrium is maintained and all is well in our market square. The market for bread and potatoes is stable and efficient.

4.3 It's Tuesday And It's Market Day – For Assets

Fast forward to Tuesday morning. The blue and white checked uniforms of the food merchants have been replaced with the pinstriped tailoring of the merchant bankers. One stall is selling stocks while another is making loans.[50] Strangely the stall selling securitised mortgage obligations is unmanned today – but let's not be distracted by detail.

As one would expect in a town devoting half of its trading time to asset markets, the townsfolk are sophisticated investors deploying a range of investment strategies. Regardless of the tactics of each strategy the aim of everyone in the market is the same: to maximise the return on their investments. And, as each investor knows, the way to maximise investment returns is through income earned from the investments and through the capital gains on the investments.

Trading begins on this Tuesday morning quietly. The brokers selling stocks are showing the same prices at which they closed business on the previous Saturday – the market appears to be in a steady equilibrium.

A small minority of the townsfolk are puritanical in their investment strategy, eschewing any form of borrowing or speculation. This group keep their money in low-risk low-yielding bank deposit accounts. At the other end of the risk spectrum is another section of the community who are active speculators routinely borrowing money for the purpose of investment. This group are happy to leverage their investment positions, provided the return generated by the investments is greater

---

[50] In today's financial markets the asset sellers are frequently also lenders who lend money to purchase the assets being sold. However, for the purpose of this story it is convenient to think of these as separate roles.

than the interest cost on the money borrowed to buy the investment.[51] Between these two extremes are another group, who consider themselves cautious, unleveraged investors; nevertheless, even these have a blend of large mortgage debts and more modest financial assets. Without being entirely aware of it this group are also leveraged investors.

Superficially, the stallholders selling stocks appear to serve the same function as the baker and farmer of the previous day's market. But appearances are deceptive. This group of merchants do something very different. In the asset markets the merchants make their living simply through buying assets at one price and then quickly selling them on at another, slightly higher, price. Accordingly the price boards on these market stalls look different to those of the baker and farmer. For every stock being traded the broker shows two prices: one is the price at which the broker will sell (offer) the asset and the other the price at which he is willing to buy (bid) the asset. Investors are therefore able to go to these stallholders both to buy and sell assets.

Another difference we have to consider between Monday and Tuesday's marketplace is the presence of the banks.[52] The bankers make their living by borrowing at one rate of interest and lending at another, higher, rate of interest. Accordingly the price boards in front of the bank stalls look somewhat similar to those of the brokers, also showing two sets of prices. The bank boards show a single price (deposit interest rate) at which the bank is willing to borrow money, and then a range

---

[51] In the language of finance, leveraged investors require a "positive carry"; income and capital gains from the asset must, on average, exceed interest costs of the loan used to buy the asset.

[52] The purpose of this section is to explain the destabilising nature of investors leverage rather than bank leverage. Therefore the effect of fractional reserve banking will be ignored, this having already been covered in Chapter 3. In practice the effect of bank and investor leverage will tend to compound one another producing a combined system with greater instability.

of interest rates at which the bank is willing to lend money. The loan rates are always higher than the deposit rate. The difference between the borrowing and lending rates reflects what the bank earns on its loans. Borrowers of the very highest standing, those considered least likely to default on their loans, are offered money at the lowest levels of interest, while those considered in a more precarious financial position are required to pay higher levels of interest.[53]

The business incentive of the banker is simple: to lend as much money as possible at the highest interest rates possible, while borrowing money at the lowest possible rate of interest. This must of course be achieved with the minimum possible risk of the loans defaulting. Clearly the twin aims of lending large amounts at high rates of interest and minimising the risk of loans defaulting are in conflict with one another. The banker therefore lives a precarious existence, grabbing for higher loan rates on

---

[53] The alert reader may have already spotted an embryonic destabilising positive feedback process in the nature of bank interest charges. Those in the weakest financial positions are also those required to pay the highest rates of interest. Once a borrower falls into a sufficiently weak financial state the bank will correctly judge that there is no viable interest rate at which a loan can be made, as the interest charge will be so onerous as to push the borrower further into insolvency. This effect is one component of a poverty trap. In some countries, America being a prime example, state-sponsored institutions have evolved to counteract this particular positive feedback – wealth polarizing – effect. The following passage is taken from the website of Fannie Mae describing its purpose and origin:

'Fannie Mae has a federal charter and operates in America's secondary mortgage market to ensure that mortgage bankers and other lenders have enough funds to lend to home buyers at low rates. Our job is to help those who house America. Fannie Mae was created in 1938, under President Franklin D Roosevelt, at a time when millions of families could not become homeowners, or risked losing their homes, for lack of a consistent supply of mortgage funds across America. The government established Fannie Mae in order to expand the flow of mortgage funds in all communities, at all times, under all economic conditions, and to help lower the costs to buy a home.'

Institutions such as these serve as valuable circuit breakers in the adverse wealth/credit-cost spiral. However, their existence can have the unfortunate side effect of artificially pushing up the cost of housing.

the one hand, while constantly nervous of default on the other. As interest rates represent a small fraction of outstanding loan values, the losses on just one defaulted loan can wipe out the potential profits on many more loans.

4.3.1 Collateralisation, marking-to-market and the calling for margin

Bankers have found ways to help them sleep more easily at night by collateralising the loans they make. This is the process whereby they lend money, but take control of assets of comparable value to secure the loan. In the event that the borrower defaults on the loan, the bank gets to sell the assets in order to repay the loan. Usually this is great business practice because the bank can lend money to buy assets, and then agree to take the same assets as collateral; as the loan has been made to pay for the assets, the assets must by definition be of a value sufficient to collateralise the loan.[54]

Collateralised lending is fine in principle but does suffer problems if asset prices fall, leaving the loan under-collateralised. In the commercial money markets the bankers have thought of a remedy for the problem of changing collateral values. Each day the value of the collateral held by the bank is checked against the prevailing market prices for the assets; this is known as "marking-to-market" and brings the bank's book value of assets into line with the latest market prices. After the marking-to-market, the new collateral valuations are checked against the bank's outstanding loans; those loans with corresponding collateral that has fallen (risen) in value are said to have become under (over) collateralised. Borrowers with under-collateralised loans are then required to provide the bank with additional assets to secure the loan.

---

[54] Home mortgages work on this collateralised loan arrangement, whereby the bank has the right to repossess the home of a delinquent mortgagee.

Generally if the borrower does not provide additional collateral, the bank will sell what collateral it has, using the proceeds to pay off as much of the outstanding loan as possible, and then pursue the borrower to pay off any shortfall.

This process of collateralised lending generates one of the key destabilising forces in financial markets. Borrowers whose assets have already fallen in value may not have additional collateral to hand, and the bank's decision to sell their collateral, into what is by definition a falling market, may simply exacerbate the borrowers' and the bank's losses. This is exactly the destabilising process that, in the current credit crisis, has caused the failure of some high-profile leveraged hedge funds.

4.3.2 Marking-to-market and credit spreads

Now consider what happens to a borrower's interest costs when his or her collateral values begin falling. The bank notices the client's losses and therefore reassesses their credit quality, which in turn leads the bank to charge higher interest rates. From the investor's perspective this is a double hit; asset prices are falling, generating capital losses, and the interest costs are rising. The resulting pressure to liquidate positions can quickly become irresistible. In debt-funded asset markets price declines beget asset sales that beget more price declines, morphing into a self-reinforcing positive feedback cycle.

The process also works in the opposite direction. As investors see their assets rise in value, their collateral positions improve, and with them their credit quality. As a result banks become willing to lend these lucky or skilful investors more money, which in turn generates additional demand for assets. In this way a virtuous cycle of price gains, increasing borrowing and further price gains is triggered – again a positive feedback cycle.

The critical difference between markets for goods and those for assets is how the markets respond to shifting prices, or equivalently shifting demand. In the goods market, higher (lower) prices trigger lower (higher) demand; in the asset market higher (lower) prices trigger higher (lower) demand. One market is a stable equilibrium-seeking system and the other habitually prone to boom-bust cycles, with no equilibrium state.

4.3.3 Investor behaviour

So far I have deliberately avoided discussing the theories of behavioural finance. This is in order to demonstrate that financial instability is hard wired into the mechanics of the asset and debt markets; it is therefore unnecessary to resort to the still-contentious arguments of behavioural finance to demonstrate market instability. But this is not to say that behavioural finance should be ignored, as this area can also give rise to powerful positive feedback cycles. Broadly speaking, investors buy assets for their income or for their potential to deliver capital gains. If an investor buys an asset in the expectation of making capital gains, the investor is, by definition, stating that he or she believes the asset to be currently undervalued. If the price of that asset starts to rise the investor's opinion will appear to be validated, and the investor will likely become more confident in the initial assessment of the asset's mis-evaluation. For this reason the investor does not necessarily sell the asset in response to its higher price, and as a result the supply of an asset does not necessarily increase with price, as would happen in the goods markets. Conversely, in the opposite direction falling prices erode confidence in the prior assessment of value triggering an increased supply of the asset. In goods markets items are purchased for consumption; in asset markets items are purchased for their potential to change price; making the nature of how the markets' participants respond to price changes fundamentally different.

4.3.4 Meanwhile, back at the town's asset market

Returning to our fictional town square asset market, we can start to pull some of these forces together. The bankers have spent their morning going through their loan books checking off the value of the outstanding loans against their client's collateral. The collateral has been marked-to-market and it's now time to call on the borrowers. Two types of messenger are sent out. For those clients unlucky enough to have collateral whose value has fallen, a polite but stern clerk is sent out with simple message:

> Send us more collateral or we will sell your assets, and hound you through the courts for all you are worth.

On the other hand, clients lucky enough to hold collateral which has risen in value are visited by a smart, smooth-talking salesperson with a different message:

> We've been looking at your holdings, and were more than a little impressed with your investment acumen. We would of course be delighted to extend you further credit should you be interested in making additional investments...and it just so happens we know a friendly broker with some splendid assets to sell you, and naturally we would be happy to take these assets as collateral against the new loan.

By the middle of the trading day the markets have settled down. The bankers have made their visits, received collateral where required and made additional loans where possible. The stallholders' prices have settled to a tranquil optimal equilibrium, as is the natural state for a truly efficient market. And, of course, each asset's price perfectly reflects its true underlying value.

Then, at about high noon, our stranger rides back into town; this time his mission is to buy shares in the town's bakery – he's heard business is picking up.

Now it so happens that our village baker is a large company worth one billion dollars ($1,000,000,000). Those one billion dollars of value are represented by one billion $1 shares.

Our stranger is a cautious fellow and is looking to buy just 100 shares. He heads off to the stockbroker's stall and notes the prices on the board. The broker is offering to sell the shares at $1.01 per share and offering to buy the same shares at $1 per share. (Earlier in the day the bankers had checked the price of the bakery's shares on the stockbroker's board, and seeing that he was willing to buy the shares for $1 had valued their client's bakery stock collateral at $1 per share.)

The stranger hands over his $101 dollars, and rides off into the sunset clutching his fistful of shares. Meanwhile the stockbroker, noting the extra demand for bakery shares, decides to increase the prices he shows on his board; he is now willing to sell bakery shares at $1.02 and is willing to buy them at $1.01 per share.

It just so happens that the banker's clerk is doing his afternoon rounds and notices the new higher prices for bakery stock. The clerk heads back to the bank to re-mark the bank's collateral to market once more.[55] The clerk reworks his calculation and finds, to his surprise, that the bank's clients are now holding an extra $10,000,000 worth of collateral. Such is the miracle of mark-to-market accounting; our stranger spends just $101 dollars and the clients of the bank are collectively $10,000,000 richer – on paper.

---

[55] To keep things simple think of this as a one-bank town, with the bank holding all one billion bakery shares as collateral. In reality, the collateral will of course be spread around many institutions and some stock will be held in unleveraged accounts. Nevertheless, the theme of the story holds.

The bank's risk systems are now showing that it can safely lend another $10,000,000; needless to say, it's time to send out the pinstriped salesmen once again. The salesmen call first on the largest shareholders of bakery stock, who are already feeling rather smug at their recent capital gain and therefore a little more confident. As it turns out, the take-up rate for the new loans on offer is poor at only 10%, but still the salesmen are able to make a new $1,000,000 loan. The investor who borrowed the $1,000,000 then goes on to spend it on more stocks.

Through the coupling of mark-to-market accounting with debt-financed asset markets, the original $101 dollar share purchase has been translated into a $10,000,000 wealth gain, an additional $1,000,000 of demand for more shares, and a banking system which thinks itself to be $9,000,000 over-collateralised.

Needless to say, once the new $1,000,000 investment is made the process begins again, potentially amplifying this purchase also into an even larger demand for stocks.

On Monday, when our stranger came into town to buy bread, his purchases displaced bread demand from the rest of the townsfolk – leaving a stable bread market. On Tuesday, our stranger's purchases of bakery stock triggered a self-reinforcing spiral of demand for stocks supported by an equally self-reinforcing spiral of debt.

Naturally, had our stranger come with the aim of selling 100 bakery shares the result could have gone in the opposite direction: $10,000,000 of destroyed wealth, margin calls, panic-selling of assets, defaulted loans and a credit crunch ultimately leading to the soup kitchens.

4.4 The Invisible Hand Is Playing Racquetball

The combination of debt-financing and mark-to-market accounting conspire to give price movements in the asset markets a fundamentally unstable positive feedback characteristic. In the goods markets Adam Smith's invisible hand is the benign force guiding the markets to the best of possible states. In the asset markets the invisible hand is playing racquetball, driving the markets into repeated boom-bust cycles.

These self-reinforcing asset-debt cycles are the essential element of Hyman Minsky's Financial Instability Hypothesis.[56] The boom-bust cycles of recent years have confirmed the presence of Minsky's destabilising credit and asset cycles time and again, yet this simple common sense analysis of why financial markets behave as they do remains a taboo subject to respectable economists.

The management of these self-reinforcing asset-credit cycles is the raison d'être of central banking. Sadly, however, this purpose is denied by mainstream economic theory, which unfortunately also provides the principles by which many of these institutions operate.

---

[56] "Stabilizing an Unstable Economy", Hyman P. Minsky, 1986.

5

Deceiving The Diligent

'Workers spend what they get, capitalists get what they spend.'

Attributed to the Polish Economist Michael Kalecki, 1899-1970

5.1 The Irrational Investor Defence

Up to this point the challenge to the Efficient Market Hypothesis has relied upon demonstrating the existence of destabilising positive feedback processes within credit and asset markets, with the power to push markets away from equilibrium. Bank credit creation, mark-to-market accounting, debt-financed asset markets, cyclical dependence of credit spreads, scarcity-driven demand and price-driven demand all provide positive feedback mechanisms with the potential to cause financial markets to behave in a way inconsistent with the theory of efficient markets. These internally generated destabilising forces could be dismissed as unimportant if it could be shown that there were even more powerful countervailing forces tending to maintain the markets in a condition of equilibrium.

According to efficient market theory the equilibrating forces which maintain market stability are generated by investors selling assets when they become overvalued and buying them when they become undervalued. Through this process, it is argued, asset prices are maintained in line with their underlying fundamental value. Returning to the example of our previous chapter, when the stranger rode into town to buy shares the additional demand initially pushed up the price of bakery stock, triggering a self-fulfilling spiral of additional demand for equities. The efficient market theory can counter this scenario by claiming that, in response to the bakery's stock becoming overvalued, other holders of the stock would be induced to sell their shares, thereby pushing stock's price back into line with its, supposedly known, underlying value.

The efficient market theory can tolerate a small temporary deviation between an asset's price and its true value provided investor activism is able to prevent the deviation persisting too long and becoming too large. Therefore, according to efficient market theory asset price bubbles are prevented by investors' appetites to buy assets on the cheap and sell them when too expensive. It follows that an asset price bubble can only be formed if investors are willing to buy assets when they are already overpriced, implying that asset bubbles require investors to behave irrationally. This line of reasoning leads to the irrational investor defence of the Efficient Market Hypothesis: to disprove market efficiency it is necessary to prove that investors behave irrationally. The following excerpt from a speech by Jean-Claude Trichet, President of the European Central Bank, describes the irrational investor defence rather well:

Are we sure asset price bubbles exist?

There is no consensus about the existence of asset price bubbles in the economics profession. Well-reputed economists claim that even the most famous historical bubbles – e.g. the Dutch Tulip Mania from 1634 to 1637, the French Mississippi Bubble in 1719-20, the South Sea Bubble in the United Kingdom in 1720 as well as the worldwide new economy boom in the 1990s – can be explained by fundamentally justified expectations about future returns on the respective underlying assets (or tulip bulbs). Thus, according to some authors, the observed price developments during the episodes that I have just mentioned – although exhibiting extremely large cycles – should not be classified as being excessive or irrational. For example, with regard to the new economy boom of the late 1990s it has been argued that uncertainty about future earnings prospects increases the share value of a company, especially in times of low-risk premia. This claim can be derived in a standard stock valuation model, where the price-dividend ratio is a convex function of the mean dividend growth rate. The mean dividend growth rate in turn depends

obviously on future expected earnings of the company.
Heightened uncertainty about future earnings will increase the
price-dividend ratio. It has further been claimed that assuming
apparently reasonable parameter values with regard to the
discount rate, expected earnings growth and most importantly
the variance of expected earnings growth, one can reproduce the
NASDAQ valuation of the late 1990s and its volatility. There
would thus be no reason to refer to a dotcom bubble. I do not
mention this example because I believe the NASDAQ valuation
of the late 1990s was not excessive. However, if one takes the
narrow definition of a bubble very often used by these economic
researchers, there is a fundamental difficulty in calling an
observed asset price boom a bubble: it must be proved that given
the information available at the time of the boom, investors
processed this information irrationally.[57]

The irrational investor argument is an ingenious construct, providing
what looks to be an impregnable defence of market efficiency. The
argument requires the doubters to prove that investors knowingly make
bad investment decisions. But of course proving that investors
knowingly make bad investment decisions is fiendishly difficult; indeed
the idea is almost an oxymoron.

However, when we look at this irrational investor argument we find
another slight of hand. Consider the last section of the quoted passage:

there is a fundamental difficulty in calling an observed asset price
boom a bubble: it must be proved that given the information
available at the time of the boom, investors processed this
information irrationally.

---

[57] "Asset price bubbles and monetary policy", Speech by Jean-Claude Trichet, President of the
ECB, Mas lecture, 8th June 2005, Singapore.

http://www.ecb.int/press/key/date/2005/html/sp050608.en.html

Is it really necessary to prove irrational investor behaviour, in order to call an asset price bubble a bubble? The questions:

- Do asset price bubbles exist?

and:

- Do investors behave irrationally?

are frequently rolled up together but are actually two quite distinct topics.

Buried deep within the Efficient Market Hypothesis is the unstated assumption that investors always have to hand the necessary information with which to calculate the correct price of an asset. If this assumption turns out to be false and investors are sometimes denied the necessary information to make informed judgements about asset prices, or worse still if they are given misleading information, then it becomes possible for asset price bubbles to form without investors behaving irrationally.

5.2 Fundamental Variables – Variable But Not Fundamental

Market efficiency requires that the prices of financial assets move in response to some known set of *externally* provided fundamental variables. The basic working model is one in which the economy does what it does, while asset prices move to reflect whatever it is that the economy is doing. That is to say, the causality runs from the economy to asset prices, and not the other way round.

If we start to relax this one-way causation and contemplate the idea that asset prices and economic fundamentals could interact via two-way causality – the economy driving asset prices and asset prices driving the economy – then a whole new set of problems open up for the idea of efficient markets; the processes through which investors are supposed to maintain the optimal equilibrium is undermined.[58]

The problem of two-way causality can be conveyed with a simple thought experiment. Consider a thermometer measuring the ambient temperature of the environment. In this system the causality runs only from the environment to the thermometer; if the environment warms up, the temperature shown on the thermometer will rise, but warming the bulb of the thermometer will not raise the temperature of the environment. For this reason it is possible to objectively assess whether the reading on the thermometer is correct; we could introduce a second thermometer to check the first, establishing if its temperature reading was correct.

Now consider what would happen if the causality between a thermometer's temperature reading and that of the environment it was measuring ran in both directions; if the environment's temperature changed, the thermometer's reading would also change, and if the thermometer's reading changed, so would the temperature of the environment.

The idea that a thermometer's reading could change the temperature of the environment is a little ridiculous, but bear with it for a while. In this new system, with bi-directional causality between environment and thermometer, the idea of an objective 'correct' temperature reading is lost; now whatever reading the thermometer happens to show is valid – the temperature of the system is unspecified by any external source. In practice such a system could meander around picking any temperature it chose, with all readings being equally valid.

---

[58] The problem of two-way causality between financial markets and economic fundamentals is a component of George Soros' theory of Reflexivity. Soros takes the argument further than is covered here, identifying still more factors contributing to Financial Market Instability. See "The Alchemy of Finance" by George Soros.

If this is all a bit abstract, consider the following question:

Was the recent housing market boom caused by, or was it the cause of, the strong prevailing economic conditions?

The variables used by investors to construct their estimates of asset value can be grouped into three classes: balance sheet, income statement and economic fundamentals. Unfortunately, all three of these sets of variables are influenced by financial markets in such a way as to undermine their ability to provide investors with objective external measures of value. Indeed, frequently these variables do not just fail to inform investors, they actively mislead them into supporting the destabilising processes described in the previous chapters.

5.2.1 Beware the balance sheet

The problems of using balance sheet information for the valuation of financial markets are the easiest to understand. Doubtless many readers will be familiar with the time-honoured ritual of lambasting the credit ratings agencies in times of financial crises. This pantomime is the same in each cycle. As the credit expansion progresses, teams of diligent credit analysts look at the loans being made and assess these against the market value of the assets being bought. At each point in the credit expansion the loans match the value of the assets being purchased and the credit gets approved. At the aggregate level, the stock of debt in the economy grows in proportion to the valuation of the economy's assets. As a result, as an asset bubble expands, the corresponding debt stock never looks excessive. Indeed, in true bubbles borrowers frequently have difficulty borrowing fast enough to keep pace with their rising asset prices, and as a consequence leverage ratios frequently improve as a bubble progresses. Time and again the observation that these leverage ratios are dependent upon rising asset prices is missed; even up to the very peak in the recent housing bubble naive analysts were citing improving household balance sheets as a reason to believe the mortgage borrowing binge was sustainable.

Once the cycle turns negative, however, and asset prices begin falling the stock of outstanding debt quickly looks excessive. This is, of course, followed by the inevitable credit downgrades and the time-honoured witch hunt for culprits, who are often to be found in the credit rating agencies.

Without wishing to spoil the fine sport of pin the blame on the donkey, it is useful to step back and consider why it is that the analysts get it wrong in every cycle. The problem lies in what economists call a fallacy of composition, which means that analysis valid at one level does not necessarily hold at another level. When the ratings analysts are assessing the quality of a loan, or the equity analysts are assessing the condition of a company's balance sheet, or the mortgage broker is assessing the safety of a mortgage, they evaluate each individual loan against the prevailing market prices for the loan's corresponding assets. In this procedure the tacit assumption is that the asset in question can be sold to repay the loan. At the micro level this is always a reasonable assumption. However, at the macro level this is almost never a reasonable assumption: one house can be sold to repay its mortgage, but if one million houses are sold at the same time prices will crash and the entire housing market will become under-collateralised.

Indeed, when one adds in mark-to-market accounting to balance sheet analysis one finds the very same destabilising positive feedback process that was discussed with respect to the banking and equity markets.

The careful analysis of individual balance sheets is intended to improve the quality of lending and investment decisions. At the micro level of the individual household or company this works. At the macro level of the entire economy balance sheet, analysis actually becomes a destabilising force, leading to excessive lending and financial instability.

Balance sheet variables, therefore, do not just fail to inform investors of impending economic problems, they may actively mislead them into believing conditions are safer than they really are. In predominantly debt-financed asset markets asset prices cannot be considered an independent metric of sustainable debt levels, nor can debt levels be considered an objective external variable with which to measure asset prices.

5.2.2 Credit creation creates profit

The situation is unfortunately little better when it comes to judging assets according to their income, that is to say using price/earnings ratios, revenue, dividend yield or any other measure dependent on the flow of money around the economy. To illustrate the point, imagine a very simple economy with only two companies, Company A and Company B. In this economy there are no messy complications of foreign trade, taxes or government spending. It is a very simple system where Company A makes all consumer goods, and Company B makes all the goods needed by Company A, including investment goods and raw material inputs. Everyone in the economy works for one of these two companies, and everyone spends all of their income on the goods produced by Company A. Neither borrowing nor saving is permitted anywhere in the economy, meaning that both the companies and the workers must spend all of their income in each period.

We can see how money would flow around this simple economy. Both Company A and Company B would pay their workers and, since savings are banned, all of their wages would be spent and turned into the revenue of Company A. Therefore Company A's revenue would be the sum of the wages of both its own employees and those of Company B. This means that Company A has a revenue stream larger than its own wage bill; it has a surplus equal to the wage bill of Company B. However, Company A must spend that surplus on its own inputs, which it buys from Company B. This flow of money from A to B pays the wages of Company B which in turn come back to Company A, to generate the surplus.

This is a grossly simplified model of any economy, but it serves to illustrate some important connections in the flow of money around an economy. If Company A decides to stop spending its surplus revenue with Company B, then Company B will no longer be able to pay its worker's wages. Company B's employees will stop buying Company A's goods and Company A's revenue will fall, and its surplus evaporate. The point is that the incomings and outgoings of all participants are intimately interdependent; no single agent can change behaviour without that change influencing the behaviour of others.

Now consider what happens if we relax the ban on savings, and as a result the workers decided to save, rather than spend, some of their wages. The revenue of Company A would fall, by the amount of the savings and, as a result, the combined wages of both companies would also fall by the same amount. These observations are the root of the first half of the quotation at the beginning of this chapter – 'Workers spend what they get' – if they don't spend it they don't get it.

Now consider what would happen if we introduce credit creation (negative savings) into the system. Once borrowing is permitted, workers become able to borrow money, from a bank, and to spend that money on extra goods from Company A. These extra purchases have been funded from borrowing and not wage income, and therefore the revenue of Company A is boosted without a corresponding increase in its wage bill. The decision of workers to borrow and spend flows directly through to a higher surplus at Company A. This windfall is in turn is likely to lead to greater spending on goods from Company B, who also has not increased its wage bill and would also therefore share in the windfall surplus.

This example shows how increasing the borrowing, or equivalently reducing the savings, of workers can act to boost corporate profits. The effect is not confined to borrowing by workers. In the real economy additional borrowing from whatever source will, all else unchanged, tend to boost corporate profits.[59] Of course the opposite is true of decreased borrowing, or increased savings rates, which tend to depress profits. For this reason, if a central bank is working to maximise economic activity in the current period, it will tend to try to force down the savings rate of its economy.

Any tendency for an economy to increase its savings rate will likely be associated with a profit recession, which, if working to a myopic efficient market paradigm (or risk management paradigm), will cause the central bank to counteract the effect with lower interest rates. Short-term demand management strategies, aimed at always boosting economic activity, will therefore tend to be aimed at depressing the savings rate of the economy. Unfortunately, however, a depressed savings rate leaves the economy precariously positioned to deal with future adverse shocks, to say nothing about what this strategy implies for the long-term investment and growth potential of the economy.

There is no more powerful mechanism for the short-term amplification of corporate profits than to persuade some element of the economy –

---

[59] In practice 'all else' is never unchanged: some of the additional borrowing could "leak" abroad in the form of an increased trade deficit; companies may find themselves obliged to pass some of the profit back to workers in the form of higher wages; and of course, governments may also adjust taxation. Nevertheless, as a rule, when an economy borrows to spend profits rise as a result.

government, household or corporation – to spend above its income. Conversely, there is no surer way to erode corporate profits than to permit any of these groups to save their income.

This process through which borrowing and savings drive economic activity is the essence of Keynes' famous 'paradox of thrift' and of his recommendation for fiscal stimulus. In the paradox of thrift, if one section of the economy tries to save money, it will reduce the income of another section of the economy, and this will likely find its way back to undermine the income of the original savers, leading them to further reduce their spending, causing a self-reinforcing cycle of declining activity. If, for whatever reason, the majority of agents in an economy become more risk-averse, deciding to increase their savings rate together, they could find themselves in a self-fulfilling economic contraction.

Keynes worked out that the escape route from the "paradox of thrift" was to get some agent (the government) to spend more money, thereby boosting profits, encouraging more borrowing, generating more profits, leading to a virtuous cycle of economic expansion. Keynes was concerned with finding a policy to help economies escape the Great Depression leading him to emphasise the "paradox of thrift" element of the story. Minsky, however, took Keynes' theory to the logical conclusion, arguing that borrowing can lead to a self-reinforcing positive spiral. This positive spiral could be thought of as a "paradox of gluttony" whereby higher borrowing produces higher profits, thereby ratifying the decision to borrow and spend more.

The paradox of thrift and gluttony are important because they are linked to the same credit creation process that drives asset market instability, described in the previous chapter. Importantly these cycles undermine investors' ability to form objective judgements about asset prices. The additional borrowing associated with an asset price boom will likely flow back into additional asset purchases, but part will also be converted into higher levels of debt-financed spending; in the recent housing market bubble this process was referred to as home equity withdrawal. As a result higher borrowing produces both higher profits, and higher asset prices, while falling levels of borrowing cuts both profit and asset prices. At the aggregate level corporate earnings do not always provide a reliable measure of the true "value" of the stock market.

Once one appreciates the connection between asset inflation, credit creation and profit formation it becomes apparent that price earnings ratios, revenue growth, and other such variables reliant on money flow, do not provide investors with objective external measures of asset values. Over reliance on these numbers can lead to self-reinforcing positive and negative asset price and credit cycles. Once again diligent inspection of the numbers may actively mislead investors into fuelling boom-bust cycles.

5.2.3 The macro data mirage

Needless to say, if asset-price inflation, credit creation and profit formation can form self-reinforcing cycles then these three variables can also feed back into what we refer to as the real economy. As profits and asset prices begin rising companies will feel more predisposed toward making new investments. As it turns out investment spending is also a key driver of corporate profits, with higher investment spending from one company flowing through to higher corporate profits at another; hence the 'capitalists get what they spend' part of Kalecki's quotation.[60]

---

[60] For a fuller understanding of this link see "Theory of Economic Dynamics: An Essay on Cyclical and Long-Run Changes in Capitalist Economy", M. Kalecki. Part 2 presents a useful framework for the analysis of corporate profits from the macroeconomic perspective, showing clearly how higher investment spending flows through to higher corporate profits.

Higher investment spending also implies higher employment, stronger consumer confidence, a greater willingness to borrow money and, therefore, stronger retail sales and economic growth figures. The upshot of all of these linkages is that asset inflation and credit expansion flow back into the real economy, generating self-ratifying stronger economic data. Unfortunately the converse is also true; credit contraction undermines profits, reduces investment spending, weakens employment, cuts consumption, and therefore creates conditions ripe for still more credit contraction – Keynes' paradox of thrift.

According to the ideas of efficient markets, asset prices are the thermometers taking the temperature of the real economy. On closer inspection asset price movements create the weather conditions that determine the temperature of the real economy. In such a system there is no defined correct equilibrium state.

5.3 Macroeconomic Policy And Credit Creation

Through its role in asset price cycles and profit generation, credit formation (the borrowing money for either consumption or investment) lies at the heart of the financial market's fundamental instability. The ability of credit creation to boost corporate profits, thereby triggering a self-reinforcing spiral of expansion, is what makes a central bank's interest rate policy such a powerful tool for controlling economic conditions. An understanding of the significance of credit formation in the promotion of economic expansion helps explain the conflicts between the various roles of today's central banks and the Efficient Market Hypothesis. While credit is expanding the economy will tend to grow, but once credit ceases expanding economic expansion will stall, and should credit begin to contract economic activity will also contract. If the central bank perceives its role as being to maximise economic expansion it must also seek to maximise credit expansion. When working under the premise of the Efficient Market Hypothesis, where all increases in economic activity are seen as moving toward equilibrium, such a policy of promoting limitless credit creation appears reasonable. And as discussed, while the credit is expanding, there will always be a ready supply of variables to which the central bank, and others, will be able to point, suggesting that the expansion is justified. However, if the self-reinforcing credit cycles described here exist, this policy of endless credit expansion becomes dangerously destabilising. As each successive attempted credit contraction is successfully counteracted with engineered stimulus, the economy is pushed into a state of ever greater indebtedness, presenting the risk of a still more violent contraction in the future. Over time, a policy of always maximising economic activity implies a constantly increasing debt stock and progressively more fragile financial system.

5.4 Fed Policy And The US Saving Rate

Over the last couple of decades the US household savings rate has fallen steadily by roughly 10% of GDP. Arguably this trend has occurred because of an activist policy of macroeconomic management; whenever the US economy has slowed down the central bank and government has responded with lower interest rates and higher government borrowing. These policies were effective in preventing any serious economic downturns. And in turn the avoidance of serious economic downturns helped "educate" households to believe that it was safe to lower their savings rate and to borrow more money.

The lowering of the US savings rates means that, relative to where things stood twenty years ago, American households have increased their annual spending by around 10% of GDP. About half of this extra spending has found its way into an increase in US corporate profits and the other half has flowed overseas in the form of a higher US trade deficit.[61] The higher corporate profits have naturally then morphed into robust equity markets, stronger investment spending and employment growth. The lowering of the savings rate has produced its own economic climate that appears to ratify the decision to save less.

5.5 Bubbles Happen Without Irrational Behaviour

Economic booms and busts create their own economic climate, making it very difficult for those operating within the bubble to formulate objective measures of the fair value of assets and therefore the sustainable level of credit; financial markets may form bubbles without investors ever behaving irrationally, once the limitations of their knowledge is accounted for.

In order to assess the sustainability of a credit expansion it is not sufficient to ask:

Do the economic variables justify the credit expansion?

Rather it must be asked:

What would the economic variables look like without the credit expansion?

And:

Would the current level of debt be sustainable under those new conditions?

These interconnections between credit and data have been made all too clear with the events surrounding today's US housing cycle, where the

---

[61] The higher US trade deficit implies higher corporate profits for non-US companies.

collapsing mortgage market has quickly fed through into lower corporate profits, deteriorating labour markets and weakening consumer demand, etc.

The correct answer to the question:

Was the recent housing market boom caused by, or was it the cause of, the strong prevailing economic conditions?

is:

Yes.

5.6 Bubble Spotting – Credit Growth Is Key

As discussed it is an unfortunate fact of our economic environment that neither the analysis of balance sheets, income statements nor (most) macroeconomic variables will flag up the onset of an unsustainable credit bubble. Fortunately, however, there are variables that can help identify the onset of bubbles and the emergence of fragility within the financial system. The clues comes in recognising that if credit creation is running substantially ahead of economic growth then that growth is likely itself to be supported by the credit creation, and will not be sustained once the credit expansion ends.

Signals of unsustainable credit expansions can be detected directly through the monitoring of lending activity, or indirectly through the behaviour of asset price inflation. Comparing the growth in asset prices and debt with that of the economy generally helps signal problems ahead. Equally, one can observe the stock of debt as a fraction of the size of the economy and the debt service burden as a fraction of the income required to service existing debt.

Close monitoring of private sector credit conditions is also important. If lenders are lending freely, at low rates of interest, economic activity is likely strong, however the debt service burden is also likely flattered. It is necessary to consider what would happen to the debt service burden, and willingness to continue borrowing, in the event that lenders suddenly tightened standards.

Finally, it is useful to consider the split of investor returns generated by assets. If asset price inflation is unusually high, compared to the income generated by those assets, then the assets may be overvalued. In these situations it is also necessary to consider what will happen to the income levels in the event of a credit contraction. This is particularly important in the stock markets where credit creation flows so directly into both the earnings and price side of the price-earnings ratio.

Given the mechanism by which most macroeconomic data can become distorted by financial bubbles, credit creation is not just an important macroeconomic variable, it is *the* important macroeconomic variable.

6

On (Central Bank) Governors

6.1 The Wobbly Bridge

In the year 2000 a new public footbridge was opened spanning the river Thames in London. The Millennium Bridge, as it was properly known, quickly gained the nickname "The Wobbly Bridge" due to its tendency to sway from side to side in response to the footsteps of those walking across it. The bridge is a form of suspension bridge, and is designed to flex; however, its reaction to the footfall of the pedestrians was not expected. What was happening was a form of spontaneous order, generated by a positive feedback process, between the movement of the bridge and the footsteps of the pedestrians. The bridge responded to the movement of the pedestrians, and the pedestrians responded to the movement of the bridge, in such a way as to coordinate the steps of the individual pedestrians with the swaying of the bridge. As the bridge swayed the walkers were forced to step from side to side in unison causing the bridge to sway even more.

In theory, as the walkers walked they could have generated enough wobble to excite the resonance of the bridge to a point at which it tore itself apart. In practice, the problem was fixed with the addition of a damping system to the bridge's structure. The dampers, which perform the same function as a car's shock absorbers, drain a little of the energy of the resonance on each cycle, or wobble, thereby preventing the motion from building to a destructive level.

6.2 The Wobbly Economy

The positive feedback processes described in Chapters 3 and 4 coupled with the processes of Chapter 5 conspire to generate spontaneous ordering within the credit markets: the actions of borrowers influence economic activity, and economic activity influences the actions of borrowers, in such a way as to promote synchronised waves of borrowing and saving. Left unchecked these waves can develop, under their own action, into self-destructive boom-bust cycles.

The role of policymakers, governments with their fiscal policy and central banks with their monetary policy, is to perform the role of the shock absorber, taking a little energy from each of the cycles. If, however, these policymakers fail to understand their purpose and attempt to maintain economic activity as if it were permanently at the peak of the cycle they risk inadvertently amplifying the wobble.

Fixing the problem with the wobbly bridge was, in theory at least, a simple task. Damping this motion simply required that sufficiently powerful shock absorbers were anchored between points on the structure which, during resonance, tended to move with respect to one another. The bridge's fixed structure gave it a set resonant frequency and a predefined mode of motion, features which allowed the damping system to be a fixed passive system.

Credit cycles do not have a fixed frequency or mode of operation, and therefore cannot be managed by a simple passive damping system. To make matters worse the agents causing these cycles – companies and households – are able to learn to anticipate the damping process. All in all this requires a more sophisticated, adaptive, damper system.

Our central banks are able to deliver the required adaptive damping, and fortunately, thanks to the genius of James Clerk Maxwell, the science of control system theory is already well-developed and able to guide us as to how central bank policy should and should not be deployed.

6.3 The Wobbly Jet

The Eurofighter jet provides an excellent introduction to the application of control system engineering to the task of managing inherently unstable systems.

Eurofighter Typhoon has a foreplane/delta configuration which is, by nature, aerodynamically unstable. The instability of the aircraft is derived from the position of a theoretical 'pressure point' on the longitudinal axis of the aircraft....

If the pressure point is in front of the centre of gravity on the longitudinal axis, the aircraft is aerodynamically unstable and it is impossible for a human to control it.

The above passage, taken from the website of the Eurofighter consortium, describes how the designers of the Eurofighter deliberately configured the jet to be aerodynamically unstable. This trick was achieved by moving the aircraft's main control surfaces, the tail plane, onto the nose of the aircraft. The effect of this adjustment is to make the jet's flight characteristics rather like those of a dart thrown backwards through the air. The jet's natural tendency is not to fly in a straight line but flip direction, and to spin out of control, in one or another direction. The instability of the Eurofighter allows it to change direction rapidly, and if necessary to fly in an erratic unpredictable manner; a useful feature when dodging gyroscopically guided missiles.

The unfortunate side effect of this unstable design is to make the aircraft's reaction speed much faster than those of any human pilot, and as a result the plane is un-flyable by unaided human pilots. To make the plane fly in a straight line the control surfaces of the jet must be continuously adjusted and re-adjusted, within fractions of a second, repeatedly flipping the craft from spinning in one direction to spinning in the other direction. This is achieved by the jet's computer controlled fly-by-wire control system.

The fly-by-wire system works through control feedback loops. A sensor measures the deviation of the jet's actual direction relative to that of the intended direction. The control surfaces are then adjusted to turn the jet back to the desired direction. The instability of the design means that this turning motion will *always* overshoot and push the jet too far in the opposite direction. This overshoot is then corrected, within a fraction of a second, by another adjustment to the control surface. This second adjustment turns the jet back toward its original orientation, and this motion also overshoots, and the cycle is repeated.

6.4 Central Banking And The Eurofighter

According to the Financial Instability Hypothesis, if left unchecked, credit expansions will continue without limit, as will credit contractions. With boom-bust cycles of this type, economic activity passes only fleetingly through points that could be considered in any way 'optimal', and these points could never be considered as points of stable equilibrium. As a result, the economy's natural tendency is to spend the vast majority of its time with credit creation, and economic activity is either too strong or too weak.

The central bank's job is to take on the control feedback role performed by the Eurofighter's fly-by-wire system, to measure economic activity and to adjust policy as necessary. When credit creation has entered an excessive, self-reinforcing expansion the central bank's role is to tighten policy (raise interest rates) and push the economy into a self-reinforcing contraction. Once the contraction has run for long enough, the central bank's role is then to ease policy (lower interest rates) triggering a self-reinforcing expansion. As with the Eurofighter's control system, perfect stability is not possible; the best that can be achieved is to keep the system wobbling within acceptable limits.

For the central bank to correctly perform the role of control feedback system it must first appreciate the necessity of the job, and accept that both credit expansions and contractions can be excessive. It is the idea that credit expansions can be excessive that is denied by the efficient market philosophy. Then the bank must understand how to measure when a corrective impulse is needed. This measurement function requires an understanding, and monitoring, of credit creation (money supply), and the ability to disregard other variables that are influenced by the credit creation process, and therefore liable to misguide policy.

6.5 Meet Mr Maxwell

The story of the science of control system engineering began in 1868 with the publication, by James Clerk Maxwell, of a paper titled "On Governors". Maxwell's "governors" were the mechanical devices used for the automatic regulation of the speed of steam engines; he could, however, have also been talking about central bank governors.

Before getting to the details of what "On Governors" said, a little background information is in order to establish Maxwell's credibility. Maxwell was born in Scotland in 1831 and died just 48 years later. In his short life he: invented colour photography; developed the first statistical theory of physics to describe the behaviour of gases – this lead to the development of modern quantum mechanics; he then unified the theories of electricity, magnetism, and light – this theory predicted radio waves, leading to modern wireless communication, and at the same time laid the foundations of Einstein's relativity. Today, Maxwell's contribution to science is ranked easily on par with that of Isaac Newton and Albert Einstein.[62]

In 1868, Maxwell turned his attention from the great scientific challenges of his day to the study of mechanical devices that were being

---

[62] See "The Man Who Changed Everything", Basil Mahon, for an excellent summary of the achievements of James Clerk Maxwell.

developed to automatically regulate the speed of steam engines. Back in the late nineteenth century the industrial revolution was in full swing, and the problem of controlling the new steam-powered machinery was a pressing technological challenge.

The problem facing the engineers was to keep the steam engines working, at a constant speed, under conditions of variable load; it was no use powering a sawmill if the cutting blade slowed to a stop when placed into contact with the tree, and then ran out of control when left to idle.

In practice these governors, as they were known, were found to produce some unexpected behaviour. Rather than bringing the rotation speed of the machinery smoothly to the desired level, they were often found to induce dangerous erratic oscillation in the machine's speed. Over time these oscillations could grow and eventually shake the machinery to pieces. In Maxwell's words what was happening was:

> '...a dancing motion of the governor, accompanied with a jerking motion of the main shaft...'

In characteristic fashion when Maxwell approached the problem of understanding steam engine governors he did not seek just to understand how these particular systems worked; he went after the much bigger prize of understanding how all systems responded to disturbances in general.

Fortunately for the rest of us, Maxwell was a rare mathematical genius who happened to believe a problem had not been truly understood until it could be described without equations. He was therefore kind enough to distil the insight of his mathematics into a simple description of how all governors work.[63]

---

[63] "On Governors", James Clerk Maxwell, Proceedings of the Royal Society, No 100, 1868.

A GOVERNOR is a part of a machine by means of which the velocity of the machine is kept nearly uniform, not withstanding variations in the driving-power or the resistance...

I propose at present, without entering into any details of mechanism to direct the attention of engineers and mathematicians to the dynamical theory of such governors...

It will be seen that the motion of a machine with its governor consists in general of a uniform motion, combined with a disturbance which may be expressed as the sum of several component motions. These components may be of four different kinds:

1) The disturbance may continually increase.

2) It may continually diminish.

3) It may be an oscillation of continually increasing amplitude.

4) It may be an oscillation of continually decreasing amplitude.

The first and third cases are evidently inconsistent with the stability of the motion; and the second and fourth alone are admissible in a good governor.

Maxwell's paper described how any system can respond to a disturbance in only one of four different ways. Remarkably these four responses encapsulate respectively:

1.   The Financial Instability Hypothesis

2.   The Efficient Market Hypothesis

3.   Poor central bank policy

4.   Optimal central bank policy

Maxwell's second mode – a disturbance 'may continually diminish' – is none other than the Efficient Market Hypothesis: when markets are disturbed forces within the system will act so as to diminish the disturbance, returning the system back to a stable equilibrium position.

Maxwell's first mode – 'The disturbance may continually increase' – is the Financial Instability Hypothesis: when markets are disturbed forces within the system will act to amplify the disturbance, pushing the system further from equilibrium.

Both the first and second modes correspond to systems, with weak or absent governors, that are dominated by the internal behaviour of the system itself.

Where Maxwell's breakthrough came, and where control system theory was born, was in identifying and understanding the third and fourth modes of operation describing how the system could respond to a disturbance, when a "governor" was present and attempting to control to that disturbance.

6.6 Two Types Of Governor

The steam engine governors, studied by Maxwell, worked like any modern feedback control system. The governor "sensed" the rotation speed of the steam engine's drive shaft, and used that measurement to adjust the drive power applied to the shaft. If the shaft was spinning too rapidly a break was applied until it slowed down. If it were spinning too slowly the break was released until the shaft re-accelerated.

The idea of automatic regulation was simple in principle, but proved difficult to implement in practice. The engineers found that the governors would apply the breaks while the shaft was spinning too fast, causing the machine to suddenly slow down. The governor would then abruptly release the break causing a sudden re-acceleration. The desired result – to maintain the speed of rotation at a constant level – was not achieved; instead the governors tended to stamp on-and-off the break, causing the machinery's speed to swing through wild oscillations.

What Maxwell found in his equations was that both the strength and the timing, of the governor's response, was important. If the governor overreacted, stamping on the break too hard or at the wrong time, a series of oscillations of continually increasing amplitude would be generated, which would eventually shake the machinery to pieces. On the other hand, if the governor were calibrated to apply a lighter touch, at the correct point in the cycle, it was possible to guide the system toward the desired speed through a series of oscillations of continually decreasing amplitude.

The engineer's instinctive response to the oscillating systems was to build ever more powerful governors. Maxwell showed that in control systems this was frequently the wrong answer. What was required was a lighter governor: a willingness to allow the system to cycle within a tolerable range, and the patience to allow the control process to converge over several cycles.

Maxwell's paper showed that is was possible to control unstable systems, but that the control process was a subtle art, where both the timing and magnitude of the control response is important, and where perfect stability is neither attainable nor desirable.

6.7 Two Types Of Central Bank Governor

The parallels between the role of Maxwell's steam engine governors and that of the modern central bank governors is not perfect, but it is close. If, as argued, the financial markets form an inherently unstable system, the optimal "governor" mechanism should accept that perfect stability is unachievable.

Credit cycles should be allowed to operate, both in their expansion and contraction phases, with policy response being applied symmetrically to both the expansion and contraction phases of the cycle. Today we have an asymmetric governor system. During the expansion phase the response is weak and delayed, but during the contraction phase it is violent and early. The result of this asymmetric policy is to move (some) central banks from Maxwell's fourth mode of operation, which is, in his words, 'admissible in a good governor' to the third mode, which is 'evidently inconsistent with the stability of the motion'.

Old school central bankers were aware of the problems of asymmetric monetary policy. To quote William McChesney Martin, the longest serving chairman of the US Federal Reserve:

> 'The job of the Federal Reserve is to take away the punchbowl just when the party gets going.'

Taking away the punchbowl is consistent with a light, well-calibrated, type four governor. A similar ethos can be read into the "leaning into the wind" strategy, which is, occasionally sheepishly, discussed by the European Central Bankers. By contrast the strategy of "risk management paradigm", recently adopted by the US Federal Reserve bank, looks to have inadvertently generated the behaviour of a mode three governor, causing a build up of ever-larger credit cycles culminating in the current credit crunch.

Governor systems, including those of central banks, were invented to protect systems from the damaging effect of wild swings in operating conditions. Maxwell showed that with only minor miscalibration these systems can do more harm than good.

Keynes and Minsky were right in arguing that the financial system requires management, and by implication requires central banking. But Friedman was also right in worrying about policy mistakes by the central banks.

6.8 Shocks – Good Or Bad?

To the efficient market school all negative shocks are destabilising events that should be counteracted. But to the financial instability school some shocks can be stabilising events, helping reverse previous cycles of unsustainable credit creation. Once the hurdle of acknowledging financial instability is cleared, it becomes apparent that the central bank should not necessarily counteract all adverse shocks. Occasionally it may actually be useful for the central bank to generate its own shocks.

Today the central banks pride themselves on their transparency and predictability. The major central banks have adopted a pattern of behaviour whereby they pre-warn the financial markets of forthcoming policy actions. It may, however, be advisable to head in exactly the opposite direction. By mandating the bank to deliver occasional short-sharp-shocks – sudden unexpected withdrawals of liquidity – the banks may be able to perform the economic equivalent of a fire drill: testing the economy's resilience to shocks; checking the sustainability of an expansion; and identifying those institutions in the most precarious financial position. If the financial markets came to believe a policy of performing occasional "financial fire-drills" were in place both lenders and borrowers would be encouraged to achieve higher levels of self-discipline.

6.9 A Control System Perspective

Viewing the function of a central bank as a feedback control system helps clarify the tasks ahead. We must work out what it is that needs to be controlled, the acceptable range of parameters in which we wish to achieve control, the correct control signal to monitor and the optimal method of applying the control impulse.

At present we are attempting to control consumer price inflation, whereas the instability of the system arises through asset price inflation. In addition to which some central banks are wilfully ignoring credit creation (money supply growth), which is the most valuable control signal, and focussing instead on other variables that tend to give misleading signals.

If we are trying to control the wrong variable, with the wrong control signal, we have little to no chance of arriving at a strategy for delivering the correct control impulse.

7

Minsky Meets Mandelbrot

'There are known knowns. These are the things we know that we know. There are known unknowns. That is to say, there are things that we know we don't know. But there are also unknown unknowns. These are the things we don't know we don't know.'

Donald Rumsfeld

7.1 Known Unknowns

The above quote earned Donald Rumsfeld widespread ridicule, which is a shame as it is a rather subtle, elegant, and quite profound observation on the nature of uncertainty and risk. When we are asked to speculate on the outcome of rolling a dice we are faced with a very controlled type of uncertainty. We do not know which number will land face up on the dice, however we do know that the number will be: one, two, three, four, five or six. We know the range of possible outcomes and, assuming a fair dice, their relative probabilities. This knowledge allows us to calculate the entire probability distribution of all possible outcomes for a dice roll. Despite its randomness we can say quite a lot about the outcome of rolling dice:

- The result will be an integer between 1 and 6 inclusive

- All six numbers have an equal 1/6th probability

- Our best expectation for the average result of many dice rolls is 3.5

Dice rolling could therefore be characterized as a process involving one of Rumsfeld's known unknowns: the outcome is unknown, but the probability distribution of all outcomes is known.

Using the probability distribution for rolling one dice we can go on to calculate the probability distribution for the sum of the numbers shown when rolling two dice. The two dice distribution is a little more interesting; each dice can land in one of six different ways giving a combined distribution of 6x6, or 36 different possible outcomes. However, if we are only interested in the sum of the two numbers on the dice then not all of the possible outcomes are unique. Six of the 36 possible numbers sum to seven – (1,6)(6,1)(2,5)(5,2)(3,4) and (4,3). As a result, the probability of rolling a seven with two dice is 6/36 or 1 in 6. By contrast, the numbers two or twelve can only be made up in a single way – two ones (snake eyes), or two sixes (boxcars). As these numbers can be produced in only one way they each have a probability of just 1/36. The probabilities of the other possible outcomes lie between these extremes.

Rolling two dice is a considerably less certain event than rolling just one dice; the possible range of outcomes is wider and the probability of each individual outcome is generally lower. Nevertheless, when rolling two or any number of dice it is always possible to produce a fully specified probability distribution spanning all possible outcomes. The uncertainty associated with dice rolling involves only known unknowns.

As discussed in Chapter 3, the Efficient Market Hypothesis requires that it is possible to simulate asset price movements in the same way a gambler may simulate the probability distribution of flipping a series of coins. As with dice rolling, coin flipping is governed by known unknowns: 50% chance of a head, 50% chance of a tail. It follows therefore that the movements of prices should also be governed by known unknowns; we don't know how the price will change but we do know how the price can change – or so the story goes.

Today the quantitative measurement of financial risk is all pervasive through our banking, asset management and regulatory systems. These risk management systems are based on the premise of market efficiency, and the idea that we are able to determine reliable probability distributions for future asset price returns. As Northern Rock and Bear Stearns have just demonstrated, the risk distributions predicted by these systems frequently underestimate real world scenarios.

7.2 Unknown Unknowns – Knightian Uncertainty

Consider a simple dice game in which the first player is required to roll a pair of dice and to record the sum of the two numbers shown. The next player is then obliged to offer odds that the next number rolled, with the pair of dice, will be equal to or higher than the number just recorded. In this game all of the risk involves known unknowns; the probability distribution of all possible outcomes is perfectly predefined and understood before anyone is obliged to give odds.

Rational players would quickly work out the fair odds for each given scenario, and the game would be no more than a process, of passing chips back and forth across the table, based on pure chance.

Now consider a small modification to the game. The conventional dice are replaced with modified dice, whose faces have been renumbered with numbers chosen at random, from within the range one to one hundred. In this new game the players are told only the sum of the two numbers shown after each roll, and are not allowed to see the dice.

As play begins, the players would be faced with a different type of risk from that of the original game. Neither the individual outcome nor the distribution of possible outcomes would be known. They would know that the maximum possible throw would be two hundred, but that this could only happen in the unlikely event that both dice happen to have been numbered with 100 on one of their faces. Similarly, they would know the minimum possible throw, 2, could only occur in the equally unlikely event that of both dice happened to carry a 1. At the outset of play the players would know that the maximum possible range of results was between two and two hundred, but they would also know that for their particular pair of dice the true range of possibilities was likely significantly narrower. The players may also work out that their best initial expectation for the first throw would be 101, but would also expect this estimate to be unreliable. The players would be faced with unknown outcomes drawn from an unknown distribution.

This type of unknown outcome from an uncertain distribution is referred to as Knightian uncertainty after the American economist Frank Knight, who first drew the distinction between events chosen randomly from a known probability distribution and events chosen at random from an unknown probability distribution.

If the players were to play with the same randomized dice repeatedly, and were to record the frequency with which they encountered each number, they would eventually be able to build up their own empirical probability distribution of the numbers the dice were likely to produce. Over a sufficiently long period of play a diligent player would be able to produce a probability distribution for the unknown dice, allowing the game to migrate from one of unknown unknowns to known unknowns. Through careful recording, collation and analysis of the game's history it would be possible, over time, to eliminate the game's initial Knightian uncertainty.

For players gambling on the unknown probability distribution, there would be a strong financial incentive to become the first player to correctly estimate the true distribution. The player with this information would be able to offer the most accurate odds, and to know when to take advantage of other players offering poorly calibrated odds.

The aim of the modern quantitative risk management system is essentially that of eliminating Knightian uncertainty through the collection and analysis of historical data. The premise of this industry is the Efficient Market Hypothesis' teaching that future return distributions are knowable and non-Knightian.

The erratic nature of the boom-bust cycles predicted by the Financial Instability Hypothesis calls into question the whole idea that previous market behaviour can reliably be used to generate future return distributions. If a return distribution is derived during a period of an expanding credit cycle it will almost certainly be entirely unrepresentative of the return distribution produced in a contracting cycle; under the Financial Instability Hypothesis neither the shape of the asset's return distribution nor its location are known with any certainty.

Most troubling is the implied tendency for the entire probability distribution to shift at the point in which the cycle flips between self-reinforcing expansions and contractions – the so-called Minsky Moments. Unfortunately, it is at these moments when risk systems are needed most. These flips are responsible for creating the illusion of extreme 25-standard deviation events of the type mentioned in Chapter 1.

7.3 Unknown Knowns

The increasing reliance on quantitative risk management systems, developed from theories based on the premise of market efficiency, has introduced the new problem of "unknown knowns" into our financial system. Unknown knowns are the things we've convinced ourselves we know but which we do not know. The Efficient Market fallacy teaches us that we know the probability distribution of asset returns, but the reality of the self-reinforcing processes within financial markets renders these distributions reliable only in quiescent market conditions. When the markets are in the grip of a self-reinforcing cycle these distributions can suddenly fail entirely. Risk management based on the Efficient Market Hypothesis is like the proverbial chocolate teapot; it works only while not in use.

7.4 The Risk Of Risk Measurement

The unfortunate side effect of the Efficient Market Hypothesis' unknown knowns is their ability to lure financial market participants into a false sense of security. Modern risk systems produce an array of numerical reports purporting to anticipate real market events. This in turn gives bankers, investors, and regulators a sense of understanding the risk they are running. In reality, however, these systems do not know what they claim to know and therefore may serve to increase confidence to inappropriate levels.

As with mark-to-market accounting, the modern risk management system was introduced to help make the financial system safer and more stable, but may have helped add to its instability.

7.5 Introducing Mr Mandelbrot

Almost since it became fashionable to model the behaviour of asset prices as though they were driven by a series of coin flips, Benoit Mandelbrot, the mathematician who invented fractal geometry, has been arguing that the behaviour of real financial markets just don't fit with the theories of efficient markets.

Mandelbrot argues that his empirical studies of price series indicate a memory effect, whereby future market price movements have a higher probability of repeating recent behaviour than would be suggested by a purely random process:

*Of course, well-behaved price changes are not the only
assumption underlying the standard financial model. Another is
that each flip of the coin, each quiver of price, should be
independent of the last. There should be no predictable pattern on
which you could trade and profit. Alas for the financial
establishment, this is also a fairy tale...Stock prices are not
independent. Today's action can, at least slightly, affect
tomorrow's action.*[64]

Benoit Mandelbrot

7.5.1 Memory is important

One of the most fascinating aspects of Mandelbrot's analysis is his claim
to have identified evidence of markets having memory. Mandelbrot
claims to have found evidence that market behaviour is influenced by
its own recent behaviour, and evidence of a clustering effect causing
large price movements to occur in short periods of time. Neither the
memory effect nor the clustering effect can be explained by the Efficient
Market Hypothesis. However, both can help explain the "fat tails"
problem and the systematic underestimation of financial market risk
by financial risk systems.

Mandelbrot's work on financial markets should be praised for its
honesty. In the first instance because he is openly acknowledging what
others only dare whisper, that the Efficient Market Hypothesis has
already been comprehensively disproved. Secondly, it is refreshingly
scientific in its method, in the sense that it attempts to fit theory to data,
and not data to theory. That said, Mandelbrot's story has a problem; he

---

[64] "The (Mis)Behaviour of Markets, A Fractal View of Risk, Ruin and Reward", Benoit B.
Mandelbrot, p98.

claims markets have memory, but does not explain where this mysterious memory comes from. If Mandelbrot's hypothesis of market memory is to be taken seriously, then the market's memory mechanism must be identified.

Efficient Market advocates insist the markets have no memory. Yet we know that every participant in the financial markets has at least some memory of their behaviour, albeit rather short in cases. We also know that financial institutions invest huge sums in databases of historic prices, and in training their staff how to use them. Memory is something that financial markets have in abundance. But this type of memory may not be the type of memory behind Mandelbrot's models; for that we may have to go back to Mr Minsky.

7.6 Minsky Meets Mandelbrot

When viewed through the lens of the Efficient Market Hypothesis, the ideas of Mr Mandelbrot seem fanciful and something to be viewed with suspicion. However, when viewed through the lens of Minsky's Financial Instability Hypothesis, Mandelbrot's ideas look logical and something to be taken quite seriously.

Mandelbrot's market memory can easily be interpreted as Minsky's self-reinforcing positive feedback processes, which also works by repeating past events as if having memory. If we wished to be precise, we could define the memory cells of Mandelbrot's theory as the balance sheets of all financial market participants. Asset price gains and losses are stored, or memorised, in these balance sheets to influence future behaviour.

Between them, the ideas of Minsky and Mandelbrot may help explain why our modern risk management industry finds it so difficult to produce reliable estimates of the future return distributions. Firstly, there is the fundamental problem that risk managers are attempting to model markets with the wrong shaped curves; normal distribution curves are most likely simply the wrong shape to simulate the behaviour of asset prices. Asset prices, driven by positive feedback, are likely to have much flatter and wider return distributions. Indeed they may frequently have double-peaked return distributions, one peak for the credit expansion cycle and another for the credit contraction cycle. Secondly, there is a problem with sampling bias: if the clustering effect that Mandelbrot proposes is real, there is a significant chance that the historic data used by risk managers to calibrate their models will not prove representative of future returns. If a period containing a cluster of positive returns is used to calibrate the model, then when the negative cluster arrives the distribution will prove hopelessly inadequate; the model will be missing one of the possible peaks of the distribution.

The problem of finding that carefully estimated probability distributions are in entirely the wrong place is sufficiently common to have been given the name of "regime shift". We have just witnessed a regime shift event in the US housing market, where lots of carefully crafted house-price return distributions have been found to be in the wrong place.

Hyman Minsky said 'stability creates instability' referring to our tendency to build up an unsustainable stock of debt in times of plenty only for that debt to then destroy the times of plenty. The issues raised here suggest a similar self-defeating problem could be at work in the quantitative risk management industry. As described previously, the role of the industry is to minimize Knightian uncertainty. However, if the industry inadvertently produces risk distributions that are systematically too narrow, there is every chance that the industry as a whole could end up encouraging excessive risk-taking, and excessive swings in risk appetite.

We now have "unknown knowns"; these are the things we don't know, but which we delude ourselves into thinking we do know.

7.7 Altogether Now

Another problematic aspect of our increasing reliance on quantitative risk management systems is their tendency to signal increased risk just after a market crash rather than before it. The upshot of this process is that once an asset has already fallen sharply in price, the risk system will then adjust higher its estimate of the asset's likely range of returns, making the asset appear more risky after a sharp loss than before that loss.

These risk measures are then fed into bank and investor positioning systems, generating a cascade of sell orders after an asset has already crashed in value, when objectively the risk of holding it should be lower, not higher, than previously.

The interplay of asset price movements and marked-to-market risk measures produce yet another self-reinforcing positive feedback channel with the power to trigger cascades of sell orders.

7.8 Building A Better Risk Management Process

Quantitative risk management is with us and is going to stay with us. If we are to get the most from our investment in this industry we should be aware of its limitations and the pitfalls into which it can lead us. As quantitative risk measures become increasingly enshrined in our markets, and even in our regulatory regime, we should remember that we are not dealing with the well-behaved randomness of the physical world. Mandelbrot describes the randomness permitted by the Efficient

Market Hypothesis as 'mildly random', and that shown by real markets as 'wildly random'.

Today we model the financial world as if it were governed by a procession of coin flips, but there is an overwhelming body of evidence suggesting this assumption is wrong. If we use the wrong tools, derived from the wrong theories, we should expect to get the wrong answers. As Mandelbrot argues, to get to the right answers we need nothing short of an entirely new statistic, one derived to fit real market behaviour, taking into account the real positive feedback processes operating within these markets.

While we continue to base our risk models, our regulatory regimes, our investment decisions and our macroeconomic policy on the mild randomness of efficient markets we will remain perpetually unprepared for the shocks thrown at us by the financial markets.

8

Beyond The Efficient Market Fallacy

'To kill an error is as good a service as, and sometimes even better than, the establishing of a new truth or fact'

Charles Darwin

8.1 Only the Fittest Theories Should Survive

Both the theories of evolutionary biology and economics are built on the common premise of progress generated by competition. Darwin's theory of evolution explains how competitive forces drive natural selection. Economic theorists, who got to the idea first, use essentially the same idea explaining how economic progress is generated through the pursuit of self-interest.

Competition is, without a shadow of a doubt, the engine of economic progress, but the engine is not the whole story. Adam Smith's pursuit of self-interest is surely the same ubiquitous a process as that of Darwin's survival of the fittest. Yet, biologists can point to a universality of evolutionary progress – wherever there is life there is evolution – whereas economists cannot say the same of economic progress; the human story shows economic development to be an ephemeral state, confined to narrow slices of history and geography. The laissez-faire philosophy of competition can be invoked to explain progress when it happens, but cannot explain a lack of progress when it fails to materialise.

We tend to consider today's explosive economic growth as the normal condition, but in truth the last few hundred years of human history have been quite exceptional when compared to the preceding several hundred thousand years of economic stagnation. And even in these years of rapid development the progress has been confined, until recently, into only narrow portions of the globe.

The prevailing laissez-faire, efficient-market orthodoxy cannot explain the historical pattern of economic progress, nor can it explain the emergence of financial crises, the behaviour of asset markets, the necessity of central banking, or the presence of inflation. In short, our economic theories do not explain how our economies work. The scientific method requires, first and foremost, that theories be constructed to accord with facts. On this count the economic orthodoxy does not qualify as a science.

If we are to progress toward an improved, less crisis-prone, system of macroeconomic management, we must first understand how our financial system really works and not how academics would like it to work. This requires the adoption of the scientific method; we must twist the theories to fit the facts, not the other way round. Theories, such as the Efficient Market Hypothesis, which fail to pass this most fundamental of tests, should be cast unceremoniously aside.

8.2 Minsky – Time For A New Hypothesis

Keynes set out on the path of finding a viable alternative to the Efficient Market Hypothesis; Minsky took us further down the same path. Minsky's theory, with financial markets flipping between self-reinforcing expansions and contractions, explains real financial market behaviour. Until better ideas come along we should adopt the Financial Instability Hypothesis as our working assumption of how our financial system really works. We should then use this as a starting point from which to consider how best to reform our macroeconomic policies.

8.2.1 Maxwell – time for a new monetary policy

Once we have accepted the wisdom of Minsky's Financial Instability Hypothesis, it is then only a short step toward understanding that credit cycles require management. This realisation opens the door to drawing upon the insight of Maxwell's control system theory.

Maxwell shows us how it is possible to over-govern a system leading to wild destructive swings in activity. We should draw upon this insight and seek to implement a minimalist approach to macroeconomic and monetary policies.

For a system as inherently unstable as the financial markets, we should not seek to achieve perfect stability; arguably it is this objective that has led to today's problems. A more sustainable strategy would involve permitting, and at times encouraging, greater short-term cyclicality, using smaller, more-frequent downturns to purge the system of excesses. In this way, it may be possible to avoid the wrenching crises of the type we find ourselves currently in. To achieve this policy would require recognition of the importance of curtailing both excessive credit creation and excessive credit destruction, and a reappraisal of our attitude to central bank policy and economic cycles. Ideally we should move beyond considering all economic contractions as symptomatic of policy failure, viewing them instead as a normal part of the operation of a healthy vibrant economy.

We should aim to achieve part of this improved stability through encouraging greater self-discipline on the part of financial market participants. In this respect, a clear message explaining the limitations of over-reliance on certain macroeconomic variables, and the value of others, would be useful; the significance of monitoring credit creation must be stressed, while the value of balance sheet analysis, and credit-driven profit formation, amongst others, should be downplayed. If, in addition, the markets were encouraged to believe that the central bank was willing to act pre-emptively to halt a credit expansion, and to delay its efforts in reversing a contraction, the markets may then learn to manage their own affairs a little better. Some creative ambiguity in central bank policy may also be useful; today's competition between central banks to be seen as the most transparent institution may be heading in the wrong direction.

8.2.2 Mandelbrot – time for new statistics

As a further step we need nothing short of complete new statistics for financial markets. Our conventional Gaussian statistics, based on the idea of entirely random price movements, is demonstrably unfit for purpose. For the analysis of financial market risk we require a new suite of tools, able to describe a pattern of asset returns under the influence of erratic self-reinforcing systems. In building these new statistics the work of Mandelbrot may prove a useful starting point.

Between the combined insight of the M3 – Minsky, Maxwell and Mandelbrot –there is every reason to believe we already have the foundations of a more realistic philosophy of financial markets, one which if applied through our existing central bank governor system should be easily able to produce a less crisis-prone macroeconomic climate.

8.3 Practical Steps

Unravelling the confusion within our academic framework is only a stepping-stone toward achieving tangible policy reform. To achieve this we must also unravel the confused and sometimes conflicting objectives facing central bank policy makers.

8.3.1 Debt drives inflation

The fundamental difference between cyclical inflation, caused by waves of credit creation and destruction within the private sector, and structural inflation, caused by public sector monetization, was explained in Chapter 3. Today's inflationary pressures do not stem from an innate inflationary bias of the fiat money system per se, rather it stems from the political imperative to avoid the damaging economic consequences of any contracting credit cycle. It is our inability to stomach even the most modest of economic downturns that feeds the Inflation Monster.

The inflationary mechanism is quite simple. Through the private sector it plays out as follows: as a credit expansion unfolds, the laissez-faire efficient market consensus is invoked to allow expansion to run for as long as possible, encouraging the maximum achievable accumulation of debt; then, once the credit cycle slips into reverse there is an immediate call for state aid – as a rule we favour capitalism in an expansion and socialism in a contraction.

The aid may come about either through accepting the debt onto the state balance sheet and then printing money to pay off the debt, or through printing money for distribution to those in debt, or by printing money to spend in other areas of the economy. All these policies amount to the same process of paying off the debt stock through a retrospective taxation on the prudent (savers) for the benefit of the imprudent (borrowers and lenders). Alternatively, the same process may, and often is, triggered without the interference of the private sector: governments spend to a point at which the central bank must acquiesce to the printing press. The whole process is described rather elegantly by Alan Greenspan himself:

> *Historically, societies that seek high levels of instant gratification and are willing to borrow against future income to achieve it have more often than not suffered inflation and stagnation. The economies of such societies tend to run larger government budget deficits financed with fiat money from the printing press.[65]*

---

[65] "The Age of Turbulence: Adventures in a New World", Alan Greenspan, 2007, p255.

It is therefore important to recognise that the threat to price stability comes about through the accumulation of debt to a point where its subsequent monetization becomes inevitable. If the debt stock is managed prudently, such that monetization policies become unnecessary, the inflation problem will evaporate and longer-term price stability will be achievable.

> *Many of the greatest economic evils of our time are the fruits of risk, uncertainty, and ignorance...Yet the cure lies outside the operations of individuals; it may even be to the interest of individuals to aggravate the disease. I believe the cure for these things is partly to be sought in the deliberate control of the currency and of the credit by a central institution...*[66]

John Maynard Keynes

For this reason, the primary focus of the central bank should be to prevent the economy accumulating an excessive unmanageable debt stock. If this can be achieved, the central bank mandates of long-term price stability and financial stability will become one.

Of course, this policy is much easier to state than to execute; an overly vigorous policy of debt containment would also be damaging to economic growth. Still, we cannot hope to rise to the challenge of macroeconomic management without first working out to what we should be aspiring.

---

[66] The passage is taken from "The End of Laissez-Faire", an essay in which Keynes argues that our economic system can be made more productive through a considered management of amongst other things both of the currency and credit systems and of the aggregate savings rate. The essay was based upon lectures delivered in 1924 and 1926, prior to the debt-deflation induced depression of the 1930s.

8.3.2 Discard consumer price targeting

The targeting of consumer price inflation by central banks leads to some perverse policy moves. In the late 1990s and early part of this decade, inflation in the Western economies was depressed by cheap exports from the industrialising economies. This lower inflation prompted the central banks to lower their interest rates: more affordable goods were met with more affordable money. Demand was stimulated by monetary policy when the supply of cheap goods was already stimulating demand. Now the situation is reversing, as emerging economies have begun driving up inflation through higher commodity prices. Rigid adherence to consumer price targeting, in this environment, risks compounding the error; as goods become more expensive so does the cost of borrowing money.

A better policy would surely have been to have had higher interest rates while our economies were receiving the windfall gift of cheap imports, allowing us to now have lower rates as we suffer the surprise tax of higher commodity prices.

The conflict between consumer price targeting and the management of credit can be easily resolved by dispensing with consumer price targeting altogether. As discussed, if excess credit and monetization is avoided, inflation will look after itself. In practical terms this move would mean shifting our central bank's mandate from targeting consumer price inflation to that of targeting asset price inflation. Put differently, the central bank would be moving its focus from the management of inherently stable goods markets to inherently unstable capital markets – if we are going to have a governor we can at least attach it to that part of the machine whose motion requires governing.

For all practical purposes this policy amounts to asking central banks to pre-emptively prick asset price bubbles, not immediately as they begin forming, but before their associated debt stock becomes so large as to demand monetization. That is, before the bubble reaches a point at which its bursting becomes a systemic risk to the economy.[67]

8.3.3 Adopt fiscal oversight

As noted, the impetus to monetize can come about through either public or private sector profligacy. If the central bank is to maintain price stability and financial stability, through the avoidance of excessive debt, it must have oversight of both private sector and public sector borrowing.

We have already recognised that the constant temptation to manipulate monetary policy for political gain requires the removal of this area of policy from the control of elected politicians. The same case could be made for fiscal policy, where the temptation for those in office to tailor spending to achieve short-term political advantage, rather than long-term economic progress, is equally powerful.

In an ideal world there would be firm controls over government budgets preventing deficit spending in all but emergency conditions. These controls would free the central bank from having to worry about the government deficit channel of monetization, allowing them to concentrate solely on the private sector. In practice, such rigid controls over government spending look unachievable. If, in return for relieving

---

[67] The arguments against asking a central bank to prick asset price bubbles are well-rehearsed, and largely fallacious. Asking a central bank to take action against excessive credit creation does not require the identification of the correct price of assets, any more than asking the bank to target consumer price inflation requires an assessment of the correct price of a can of baked beans. Both policies require an assessment of what is and is not a reasonable rate of price change, but neither requires an assessment of price level. If the central bank cannot detect the formation of a bubble such as the one just witnessed, we must question its ability to detect any economic disturbance worthy of policy action. If central banks cannot spot asset price bubbles, it may be better to follow Friedman's advice, and to shut up shop altogether.

the banks of the need to target consumer price inflation, the central banks were given the job of policing the fiscal position of government, we may arrive at a better-combined policy. Central banks could perhaps present an annual assessment of the government's fiscal position, and demand, where necessary, the government respond with any corrective action that may be required. Such a mechanism would be far from perfect, but it would at least give the central bank some influence over polices likely to destabilise the monetary system. At the same time it would also help coordinate the implementation of fiscal and monetary stimulus policies, when used, and add a welcome layer of discipline to government spending.

8.4 Near Term Options – 1970s, 1930s Or Yet Another Bubble

As things stand today, the combined debt stock, accumulated through the procession of bubbles stretching back two or more decades, is almost certainly already unsustainable. Broadly speaking, this situation leaves us with one of three unpalatable options:

1. **The free market route**

    Allow the credit contraction and asset deflation to run its course. This "purge the rottenness" out of the system strategy was famously advocated by Andrew Mellon in response to the Great Depression when he argued to: 'Liquidate labor, liquidate stocks, liquidate the farmers, liquidate real estate.' Such a strategy would almost certainly lead to another great depression and would therefore be, to say the least, inadvisable.

2.   **When in trouble double**

Alternatively we could attempt to encourage yet another massive debt-fuelled spending spree, using fiscal and monetary stimulus, in the hope of triggering another self-reinforcing expansion, with sufficient power to negate the current contraction. In the short term, this strategy would appear more palatable than the free market solution. However, this is precisely the short-sighted strategy that was used to deal with the aftermath of the 1990s corporate borrowing binge and led directly to today's crisis. Even if we could find another credit bubble to inflate, a further layer of debt-fuelled spending would only delay and amplify the problems. This strategy is also inadvisable.

3.   **Unleash the Inflation Monster**

The third option is to engage the printing press. Use the printing press to pay off the outstanding stock of debt, either directly with state handouts or indirectly with inflationary spending policies. This strategy gives borrowers a "get out of jail free card", paid for at the expense of savers. This strategy is also deeply unpalatable, but is nevertheless the least inadvisable of the three available options. The recent oil, gold, and food price rises, together with the falling value of the US dollar, are almost certainly signs of this strategy being both anticipated and deployed.

In deploying the Inflation Monster strategy we should not pretend to be doing anything other than engaging in retrospective taxation for the purpose of redistributing wealth. In the long run the boom-inflate cycle threatens not just price stability but also undermines property rights, thereby striking at the very heart of capitalism.

It is both a strength and a weakness of the fiat money system that such an exit strategy is available. We will, most likely, be able to avoid the wrenching dislocations of the 1930s. But at the same time the availability of this escape path has promoted cavalier conduct leading up to this crisis. From this starting point unshackling the Inflation Monster is probably the right thing to do. Thereafter, it is imperative we move forward to build a more informed and sustainable strategy for monetary and macroeconomic policy and one that does not lead us immediately back to the current situation.

9

Concluding Remarks

In today's climate, the arguments I have presented here will doubtless be interpreted as a narrowly targeted criticism of the recent policies of the US Federal Reserve bank. Unfortunately, this conclusion cannot be avoided, as without doubt the analysis suggests US monetary policy has played a significant role in the incubation of today's crisis. That said, it would be entirely wrong to lay blame at the feet of any one institution, much less any one individual. The policy strategies of our central banks are largely determined by the prevailing economic wisdom of the day and, of late, that wisdom has generally failed to identify the necessity of managing aggregate credit creation.[68] What's more, we should not neglect the role of Japanese monetary policy in this story. As a direct result of the same type of policy errors described here, the Japanese borrowing binge of the 1980s has been converted into a thirteen-year long period of zero or near-zero Japanese interest rates. The persistence of such low rates for such a long period within such an important, export-driven economy has undoubtedly played a significant role in today's malaise.

If blame must be laid anywhere it must be placed at the collective feet of the academic community for having chosen to continue promoting their flawed theories of efficient, self-regulating markets, in the face of overwhelming contradictory evidence.

Credit creation is the foundation of the wealth-generation process; it is also the cause of financial instability. We should not allow the merits of the former to blind us to the risks of the latter. We are lucky enough to have inherited the best monetary and financial architecture in history. The system comes complete with a central banking system, which, if

---

[68] To their credit, in the face of significant criticism, the ECB has stuck to its second pillar of monetary policy, which stresses the importance of money supply growth for central bank policy.

used properly, should be able to contain the inherent instability of our credit system, and thereby enhance our long-term wealth-generating capacity.

The practical steps needed to turn this governor system from Maxwell's destabilising third mode of operation to his stabilising fourth mode are trivial. The greater challenge lies in changing our mindset from one of unquestioning faith in market efficiency to one that accepts the need for governance of aggregate credit creation, and the occasional tough choices that this requires.

Appendix

ON GOVERNORS

J.C. MAXWELL

From the Proceedings of the Royal Society, *No.100, 1868.*

A GOVERNOR is a part of a machine by means of which the velocity of the machine is kept nearly uniform, notwithstanding variations in the driving-power or the resistance.

Most governors depend on the centrifugal force of a piece connected with a shaft of the machine. When the velocity increases, this force increases, and either increases the pressure of the piece against a surface or moves the piece, and so acts on a break or a valve.

In one class of regulators of machinery, which we may call *moderators*[1], the resistance is increased by a quantity depending on the velocity. Thus in some pieces of clockwork the moderator consists of a conical pendulum revolving within a circular case. When the velocity increases, the ball of the pendulum presses against the inside of the case, and the friction checks the increase of velocity.

In Watt's governor for steam-engines the arms open outwards, and so contract the aperture of the steam-valve.

In a water-break invented by Professor J. Thomson, when the velocity is increased, water is centrifugally pumped up, and overflows with a great velocity, and the work is spent in lifting and communicating this velocity to the water.

In all these contrivances an increase of driving-power produces an increase of velocity, though a much smaller increase than would be produced without the moderator.

But if the part acted on by centrifugal force, instead of acting directly on the machine, sets in motion a contrivance which continually increases the resistance as long as the velocity is above its normal value, and reverses its action when the velocity is below that value, the governor will bring the velocity to the same normal value whatever variation (within the working limits of the machine) be made in the driving-power or the resistance.

I propose at present, without entering into any details of mechanism to direct the attention of engineers and mathematicians to the dynamical theory of such governors.

It will be seen that the motion of a machine with its governor consists in general of a uniform motion, combined with a disturbance which may be expressed as the sum of several component motions. These components may be of four different kinds :-

(1) The disturbance may continually increase.

(2) It may continually diminish.

(3) It may be an oscillation of continually increasing amplitude.

(4) It may be an oscillation of continually decreasing amplitude.

---

[1]See Mr C. W. Siemens "On Uniform Rotation,"*Phil. Trans.* 1866, p. 657.

1

The first and third cases are evidently inconsistent with the stability of the motion; and the second and fourth alone are admissible in a good governor. This condition is mathematically equivalent to the condition that all the possible roots, and all the possible parts of the impossible roots, of a certain equation shall be negative.

I have not been able completely to determine these conditions for equations of a higher degree than the third; but I hope that the subject will obtain the attention of mathematicians.

The actual motions corresponding to these impossible roots are not generally taken notice of by the inventors of such machines, who naturally confine their attention to the way in which it is designed to act; and this is generally expressed by the real root of the equation. If, by altering the adjustments of the machine, its governing power is continually increased, there is generally a limit at which the disturbance, instead of subsiding more rapidly, becomes an oscillating and jerking motion, increasing in violence till it reaches the limit of action of the governor. This takes place when the possible part of one of the impossible roots becomes positive. The mathematical investigation of the motion may be rendered practically useful by pointing out the remedy for these disturbances.

This has been actually done in the case of a governor constructed by Mr Fleeming Jenkin, with adjustments, by which the regulating power of the governor could be altered. By altering these adjustments the regulation could be made more and more rapid, till at last a dancing motion of the governor , accompanied with a jerking motion of the main shaft, shewed that an alteration had taken place among the impossible roots of the equation.

I shall consider three kinds of governors, corresponding to the three kinds of moderators already referred to.

In the first kind, the centrifugal piece has a constant distance from the axis of motion, but its pressure on a surface on which it rubs varies when the velocity varies. In the moderator this friction is itself the retarding force. In the governor this surface is made moveable about the axis, and the friction tends to move it; and this motion is made to act on a break to retard the machine. A constant force acts on the moveable wheel in the opposite direction to that of the friction, which takes off the break when the friction is less than a given quantity.

Mr Jenkin's governor is on this principle. It has the advantage that the centrifugal piece does not change its position, and that its pressure is always the same function of the velocity. It has the disadvantage that the normal velocity depends in some degree on the coefficient of sliding friction between two surfaces which cannot be kept always in the same condition.

In the second kind of governor, the centrifugal piece is free to move further from the axis, but is restrained by a force the intensity of which varies with the position of the centrifugal piece in such a way that, if the velocity of rotation has the normal value, the centrifugal piece will be in equilibrium in every position. If the velocity is greater or less than the normal velocity. the centrifugal piece will fly out or fall in without any limit except the limits of motion of the piece. But a break is arranged so that it is made more or less powerful according to the distance of the centrifugal piece from the axis, and thus the oscillations of the centrifugal piece are restrained within narrow limits.

Governors have been constructed on this principle by Sir W. Thomson and by M. Foucault. In the first, the force restraining the centrifugal piece is that of a spring acting between a point of the centrifugal piece and a fixed point at a considerable distance, and the break is a friction-break worked by the reaction of the spring on the fixed point.

In M. Foucault's arrangement, the force acting on the centrifugal piece is the weight of the balls acting downward, and an upward force produced by weights acting on a combination of levers and tending to raise the balls. The resultant vertical force on the balls is proportional to their depth below the centre of motion, which ensures a constant normal velocity. The break is :- in the first place, the variable friction between the combination of levers and the ring on the shaft on which the force is made to act; and, in the second place, a centrifugal air-fan through. which more or less air is allowed to pass, according to the, position of the levers. Both these causes tend to regulate the velocity according to the same law.

The governors designed by the Astronomer-Royal on Mr Siemens's principle for the chronograph and equatorial of Greenwich Observatory depend on nearly similar conditions. The centrifugal piece is here a long conical pendulum, not far removed from the vertical, and it is prevented from deviating much from a fixed angle by the driving-force being rendered nearly constant by means of a differential system. The break of the pendulum consists of a fan which dips into a liquid more or less, according to the angle of the pendulum with the vertical. The break of the principal shaft is worked by the differential apparatus; and the smoothness of motion of the principal shaft is ensured by connecting it with a fly-wheel.

In the third kind of governor a liquid is pumped up and thrown out over the sides of a revolving cup. In the governor on this principle, described by Mr C. W. Siemens, the cup is connected with its axis by a screw and a spring, in such a way that if the axis gets ahead of the cup the cup is lowered and more liquid is pumped up, If this adjustment can be made perfect, the normal velocity of the cup will remain the same through a considerable range of driving-power.

It appears from the investigations that the oscillations in the motion must be checked by some force resisting the motion of oscillation. This may be done in some cases by connecting the oscillating body with a body hanging in a viscous liquid, so that the oscillations cause the body to rise and fall in the liquid.

To check the variations of motion in a revolving shaft, a vessel filled wit 1h viscous liquid may be attached to the shaft. It will have no effect on uniform rotation, but will check periodic alterations of speed.

Similar effects are produced by the viscosity of the lubricating matter in the sliding parts of the machine, and by other unavoidable resistances; so that it is not always necessary to introduce special contrivances to check oscillations.

I shall call all such resistances, if approximately proportional to the velocity, by the name of "viscosity", whatever be their true origin.

In several contrivances a differential system of wheel-work is introduced between the machine and the governor, so that the driving-power acting on the governor is nearly constant.

I have pointed out that, under certain conditions, the sudden disturbances of the machine do not act through the differential system on the governor, or vice versa. When these conditions are fulfilled, the equations of motion are not only simple, but the motion itself is not liable to disturbances depending on the mutual action of the machine and the governor.

DISTINCTION BETWEEN MODERATORS AND GOVERNORS.

In regulators of the first kind, let P be the driving-power and R the resistance, both estimated as if applied to a given axis of the machine. Let V be the normal velocity, estimated for the same axis, and dx/dt the actual velocity, and let M be the moment of inertia of the whole machine reduced to the given axis.

Let the governor be so arranged as to increase the resistance or diminish the driving-power by a quantity $F(dx/dt - V)$, then the equation of motion will be

$$(1) \qquad \frac{d}{dt}\left(M\frac{dx}{dt}\right) = P - R - F\left(\frac{dx}{dt} - V\right)$$

When the machine has obtained its final rate the first term vanishes, and

$$(2) \qquad \frac{dx}{dt} = V\frac{P-R}{F}$$

Hence, if P is increased or R diminished, the velocity will be permanently increased. Regulators of this kind, as Mr Siemens [2], has observed, should be called moderators rather than governors.

In the second kind of regulator, the force $F(dx/dt - V)$, instead of being applied directly to the machine, is applied to an independent moving piece, B, which continually increases the resistance, or diminishes the driving-power, by a quantity depending on the whole motion of B.

If y represents the whole motion of B, the equation of motion of B is

$$(3) \qquad \frac{d}{dt}\left(B\frac{dy}{dt}\right) = F\left(\frac{dx}{dt} - V\right)$$

and that of M

$$(4) \qquad \frac{d}{dt}\left(M\frac{dx}{dt}\right) = P - R - F\left(\frac{dx}{dt} - V\right) + Gy$$

where G is the resistance applied by B when B moves through one unit of space.

We can integrate the first of these equations at once, and we find

$$(5) \qquad B\frac{dy}{dt} = F(x - Vt)$$

so that if the governor B has come to rest $x = Vt$, and not only is the velocity of the machine equal to the normal velocity, but the position of the machine is the same as if no disturbance of the driving-power or resistance had taken place.

Jenkin's Governor. In a governor of this kind, invented by Mr Fleeming Jenkin, and used in electrical experiments, a centrifugal piece revolves on the principal axis, and is kept always at a constant angle by an appendage which slides on the edge of a loose wheel, B, which works on the same axis. The pressure on the edge of this wheel would be proportional to the square of the velocity; but a constant portion

---

[2]"On Uniform Rotation," *Phil. Trans.* 1866, p. 657.

of this pressure is taken off by a spring which acts on the centrifugal piece. The force acting on B to turn it round is therefore

$$F' \left[\frac{dx}{dt} \right]^2 - C';$$

and if we remember that the velocity varies within very narrow limits, we may write the expression

$$F \left(\frac{dx}{dt} - V_1 \right);$$

where F is a new constant, and V_1 is the lowest limit of velocity within which the governor will act.

Since this force necessarily acts on B in the positive direction, and since it is necessary that the break should be taken off as well as put on, a weight W is applied to B tending to turn it in the negative direction; and, for a reason to be afterwards explained, this weight is made to hang in a viscous liquid, so as to bring it to rest quickly.

The equation of motion of B may then be written

$$(6) \qquad B\frac{d^2y}{dt^2} = F \left(\frac{dx}{dt} - V_1 \right) - Y\frac{dy}{dt} - W,$$

where Y is a coefficient depending on the viscosity of the liquid and on other resistances varying with the velocity, and W is the constant weight.

Integrating this equation with respect to t, we find

$$(7) \qquad B\frac{dy}{dt} = F(x - V_1 t) - Yy - Wt$$

If B has come to rest, we have

$$(8) \qquad x = \left(V_1 + \frac{W}{F} \right) t + \frac{Y}{F}y,$$

or the position of the machine is affected by that of the governor, but the final velocity is constant, and

$$(9) \qquad V_1 + \frac{W}{F} = V,$$

where V_1 is the normal velocity.

The equation of motion of the machine itself is

$$(10) \qquad M\frac{d^2x}{dt^2} = P - R - F \left(\frac{dx}{dt} - V_1 \right) - Gy$$

This must be combined with equation (7) to determine the motion of the whole apparatus. The solution is of the form

$$(11) \qquad x = A_1 e^{n_1 t} + A_2 e^{n_2 t} + A_3 e^{n_3 t} + Vt$$

where n_1, n_2, n_3 are the roots of the cubic equation

$$(12) \qquad MBn^3 + (MY + FB) n^2 + FYn + FG = 0$$

If n be a pair of roots of this equation of the form $a \pm \sqrt{-1}b$, then the part of x corresponding to these roots will be of the form

$$(13) \qquad e^{at} \cos(bt + \beta).$$

If a is a negative quantity, this will indicate an oscillation the amplitude of which continually decreases. If a is zero, the amplitude will remain constant, and if a is positive, the amplitude will continually increase.

One root of the equation (12) is evidently a real negative quantity. The condition that the real part of the other roots should be negative is

$$(14) \qquad \left(\frac{F}{M} + \frac{Y}{B}\right)\frac{Y}{B} - \frac{G}{B} = \text{a positive quantity.}$$

This is the condition of stability of the motion. If it is not fulfilled there will be a dancing motion of the governor, which will increase till it is as great as the limits of motion of the governor. To ensure this stability, the value of Y must be made sufficiently great, as compared with G, by placing the weight W in a viscous liquid if the viscosity of the lubricating materials at the axle is not sufficient.

To determine the value of F, put the break out of gear, and fix the moveable wheel; then, if V and V' be the velocities when the driving-power is P and P',

$$(15) \qquad F = \frac{P - P'}{V - V'}$$

To determine G, let the governor act, and let y and y' be the positions of the break when the driving-power is P and P' ,then

$$(16) \qquad G = \frac{P - P'}{y - y'}.$$

General Theory of Chronometric Centrifugal Pieces.

Sir W. Thomson's and M. Foucault's Governors. Let A be the moment of Inertia of a revolving apparatus, and θ the angle of revolution. The equation of motion is

$$(17) \qquad \frac{d}{dt}\left(A\frac{d\theta}{dt}\right) = L$$

where L is the moment of the applied force round the axis. Now, let A be a function of another variable ϕ (the divergence of the centrifugal piece), and let the kinetic energy of the whole be

$$\tfrac{1}{2}A\left[\frac{d\theta}{dt}\right]^2 + \tfrac{1}{2}B\left[\frac{d\phi}{dt}\right]^2$$

where B may also be a function of ϕ, if the centrifugal piece is complex.

If we also assume that P, the potential energy of the apparatus is a function of ϕ then the force tending to *diminish* ϕ, arising from the action of gravity, springs, etc., will be $dP/d\phi$.

The whole energy, kinetic and potential, is

$$(18) \qquad E = \tfrac{1}{2}A\left[\frac{d\theta}{dt}\right]^2 + \tfrac{1}{2}B\left[\frac{d\phi}{dt}\right]^2 + P = \int L d\theta$$

Differentiating with respect to t, we find

$$(19) \qquad \frac{d\phi}{dt}\left(\tfrac{1}{2}\frac{dA}{d\phi}\left[\frac{d\theta}{dt}\right]^2 + \tfrac{1}{2}\frac{dB}{d\phi}\left[\frac{d\phi}{dt}\right]^2 + \frac{dP}{d\phi}\right) + A\frac{d\theta}{dt}\frac{d^2\theta}{dt^2} + B\frac{d\phi}{dt}\frac{d^2\phi}{dt^2}$$

$$= L\frac{d\theta}{dt} = \frac{d\theta}{dt}\left(\frac{dA}{d\phi}\frac{d\theta}{dt}\frac{d\phi}{dt} + A\frac{d^2\theta}{dt^2}\right)$$

whence we have, by eliminating L,

$$(20) \qquad \frac{d}{dt}\left(\frac{d\phi}{dt}\right) = \tfrac{1}{2}\frac{dA}{d\phi}\left[\frac{d\theta}{dt}\right]^2 + \tfrac{1}{2}\frac{dB}{d\phi}\left[\frac{d\phi}{dt}\right]^2 - \frac{dP}{d\phi}$$

The first two terms of the right-hand side indicate a force tending to *increase* ϕ depending on the squares of the velocities of the main shaft and of the centrifugal piece. The force indicated by these terms may be called the centrifugal force.

If the apparatus is so arranged that

$$(21) \qquad P = \tfrac{1}{2}A\omega^2 + \text{const}$$

where ω is a constant velocity, the equation becomes

$$(22) \qquad \frac{d}{dt}\left(B\frac{d\phi}{dt}\right) = \tfrac{1}{2}\frac{dA}{d\phi}\left(\left[\frac{d\theta}{dt}\right]^2 - \omega^2\right) + \tfrac{1}{2}\frac{dB}{d\phi}\left[\frac{d\phi}{dt}\right]^2$$

In this case the value of ϕ cannot remain constant unless the angular velocity is equal to ω.

A shaft with a centrifugal piece arranged on this principle has only one velocity of rotation without disturbance. If there be a small disturbance, the equations for the disturbance θ and ϕ may be written

$$(23) \qquad A\frac{d^2\theta}{dt^2} + \frac{dA}{d\phi}\omega\frac{d\phi}{dt} = L,$$

$$(24) \qquad B\frac{d^2\phi}{dt^2} - \frac{dA}{d\phi}\omega\frac{d\theta}{dt} = 0.$$

The period of such small disturbances is $(dA/d\phi)(AB)^{-1/2}$ revolutions of the shaft. They will neither increase nor diminish if there are no other terms in the equations.

To convert this apparatus into a governor, let us assume viscosities X and Y in the motions of the main shaft and the centrifugal piece, and a resistance $G\phi$ applied to the main shaft. Putting $(dA/d\phi)\omega = K$, the equations become

$$(25) \qquad A\frac{d^2\theta}{dt^2} + X\frac{d\theta}{dt} + K\frac{d\phi}{dt} + G\phi = L,$$

$$(26) \qquad B\frac{d^2\phi}{dt^2} + Y\frac{d\phi}{dt} - K\frac{d\theta}{dt} = 0.$$

The condition of stability of the motion indicated by these equations is that all the possible roots, or parts of roots, of the cubic equation

$$(27) \qquad ABn^3 + (AY + BX)n^2 + (XY + K^2)n + GK = o$$

shall be negative; and this condition is

$$(28) \qquad \left(\frac{X}{A} + \frac{Y}{B}\right)(XY + K^2) > GK.$$

Combination of Governors. If the break of Thomson's governor is applied to a moveable wheel, as in Jenkin's governor, and if this wheel works a steam-valve, or a more powerful break, we have to consider the motion of three pieces. Without entering into the calculation of the general equations of motion of these pieces, we may confine ourselves to the case of small disturbances, and write the equations

$$A\frac{d^2\theta}{dt^2} + X\frac{d\theta}{dt} + K\frac{d\phi}{dt} + T\phi + J\psi = P - R,$$

(29)
$$B\frac{d^2\phi}{dt^2} + Y\frac{d\phi}{dt} - K\frac{d\theta}{dt} = 0,$$

$$C\frac{d^2\psi}{dt^2} + Z\frac{d\psi}{dt} - T\phi = 0$$

where θ, ϕ, χ are the angles of disturbance of the main shaft, the centrifugal arm, and the moveable wheel respectively, A, B, C their moments of inertia, X, Y, Z the viscosity of their connexions, K is what was formerly denoted by $dA/d\phi = \omega$, and T and J are the powers of Thomson's and Jenkin's breaks respectively.

The resulting equation in n is of the form

(30)
$$\begin{vmatrix} An^2 + Xn & Kn + T & J \\ -K & Bn + Y & 0 \\ 0 & -T & Cn^2 + Zn \end{vmatrix} = 0$$

or

(31) $$n^5 + n^4\left(\frac{X}{A} + \frac{Y}{B} + \frac{Z}{C}\right) + n^3\left[\frac{XYZ}{ABC}\left(\frac{X}{A} + \frac{Y}{B} + \frac{Z}{C}\right) + \frac{K^2}{AB}\right]$$
$$+ n^2\left(\frac{XYZ + KTC + K^2Z}{ABC}\right) + n\frac{KTZ}{ABC} + \frac{KTZJ}{ABC} = 0.$$

I have not succeeded in determining completely the conditions of stability of the motion from this equation; but I have found two necessary conditions, which are in fact the conditions of stability of the two governors taken separately. If we write the equation

(32) $$n^5 + pn^4 + qn^3 + rn^2 + sn + t = 0,$$

then, in order that the possible parts of all the roots shall be negative, it is necessary that

(33) $pq > r$ and $ps > t$.

I am not able to shew that these conditions are sufficient. This compound governor has been constructed and used.

On the Motion of a Liquid in a Tube revolving about a Vertical Axis.

Mr C. W. Siemens's Liquid Governor. Let ρ be the density of the fluid, k the section of the tube at a point whose distance from the origin measured along the tube is s, r, θ, z the co-ordinates of this point referred to axes fixed with respect to the tube, Q the volume of liquid which passes through any section in unit of time. Also let the following integrals, taken over the whole tube, be

(34) $$\int \rho k r^2 ds = A, \quad \int \rho r^2 d\theta = B, \quad \int \rho\frac{1}{\alpha}ds = C,$$

the lower end of the tube being in the axis of motion.

Let ϕ be the angle of position of the tube about the vertical axis, then the moment of momentum of the liquid in the tube is

$$(35) \qquad H = A\frac{d\phi}{dt} + BQ.$$

The moment of momentum of the liquid thrown out of the tube in unit of time is

$$(36) \qquad \frac{dH'}{dt} = \rho r^2 Q\frac{d\phi}{dt} + \rho\frac{r}{k}Q^2\cos\alpha,$$

where r is the radius at the orifice, k its section, and α the angle between the direction of the tube there and the direction of motion.

The energy of motion of the fluid in the tube is

$$(37) \qquad W = \tfrac{1}{2}A\left[\frac{d\phi}{dt}\right]^2 + BQ\frac{d\phi}{dt} + \tfrac{1}{2}CQ^2.$$

The energy of the fluid which escapes in unit of time is

$$(38) \qquad \frac{W'}{dt} = \rho gQ(h+z) + \tfrac{1}{2}\rho r^2 Q\left[\frac{d\phi}{dt}\right]^2 + \rho\frac{r}{k}Q^2\cos\alpha\frac{d\phi}{dt} + \tfrac{1}{2}\frac{\rho}{k^2}Q^3.$$

The work done by the prime mover in turning the shaft in unit of time is

$$(39) \qquad L\frac{d\phi}{dt} = \frac{d\phi}{dt}\left(\frac{dH}{dt} + \frac{dH'}{dt}\right).$$

The work spent on the liquid in unit of time is

$$(40) \qquad \frac{dW}{dt} + \frac{dW'}{dt}.$$

Equating this to the work done, we obtain the equations of motion

$$(41) \qquad A\frac{d^2\phi}{dt^2} + B\frac{dQ}{dt} + \rho r^2 Q\frac{d\phi}{dt} + \rho\frac{r}{k}\cos\alpha Q^2 = L$$

$$(42) \qquad B\frac{d^2\phi}{dt^2} + C\frac{dQ}{dt} + \tfrac{1}{2}\frac{\rho}{k^2}Q^2 + \rho g(h+z) - \tfrac{1}{2}\rho r^2\left[\frac{d\phi}{dt}\right]^2 = 0$$

These equations apply to a tube of given section throughout. If the fluid is in open channels, the values of A and C will depend on the depth to which the channels are filled at each point, and that of k will depend on the depth at the overflow.

In the governor described by Mr C. W. Siemens in the paper already referred to, the discharge is practically limited by the depth of the fluid at the brim of the cup.

The resultant force at the brim is $f = \sqrt{g^2 + \omega^4 r^2}$.

If the brim is perfectly horizontal, the overflow will be proportional to $x^{3/2}$ (where x is the depth at the brim), and the mean square of the velocity relative to the brim will be proportional to x, or to $Q^{2/3}$.

If the breadth of overflow at the surface is proportional to x^n, where x is the height above the lowest point of overflow, then Q will vary as $x^{n+3/2}$, and the mean square of the velocity of overflow relative to the cup as x or as $1/Q^{n+3/2}$.

If $n = -1/2$, then the overflow and the mean square of the velocity are both proportional to x.

From the second equation we find for the mean square of velocity

$$(43) \qquad \frac{Q^2}{k^2} = -\frac{2}{\rho}\left(B\frac{d^2\phi}{dt^2} + C\frac{dQ}{dt}\right) + r^2\left[\frac{d\phi}{dt}\right]^2 - 2g(h+z)$$

If the velocity of rotation and of overflow is constant, this becomes

$$(44) \qquad \frac{Q^2}{k^2} = r^2 \left[\frac{d\phi}{dt}\right]^2 - 2g(h+z)$$

From the first equation, supposing, as in Mr Siemens's construction, that $\cos \alpha = 0$ and $B = 0$, we find

$$(45) \qquad L = \rho r^2 \frac{d\phi}{dt}$$

In Mr Siemens's governor there is an arrangement by which a fixed relation is established between L and z,

$$(46) \qquad L = -Sz$$

whence

$$(47) \qquad \frac{Q^2}{k^2} = r^2 \left[\frac{d\phi}{dt}\right]^2 - 2gh + 2\frac{g\rho}{S}r^2 Q \frac{d\phi}{dt}$$

If the conditions of overflow can be so arranged that the mean square of the velocity, represented by Q^2/k^2, is proportional to Q, and if the strength of the spring which determines S is also arranged so that

$$(48) \qquad \frac{Q^2}{k^2} = 2\frac{g\rho}{S}r^2 \omega Q$$

the equation will become, if $2gh = \omega^2 r^2$,

$$(49) \qquad 0 = r^2 \left(\left[\frac{d\phi}{dt}\right]^2 - \omega^2\right) + 2\frac{g\rho}{S}r^2 Q \left(\frac{d\phi}{dt} - \omega\right),$$

which shews that the velocity of rotation and of overflow cannot be constant unless the velocity of rotation is ω.

The condition about the overflow is probably difficult to obtain accurately in practice; but very good results have been obtained within a considerable range of driving-power by a proper adjustment of the spring. If the rim is uniform, there will be a *maximum* velocity for a certain driving-power. This seems to be verified by the results given at p. 667 of Mr Siemens's paper.

If the flow of the fluid were limited by a hole, there would be a *minimum* velocity instead of a maximum.

The differential equation which determines the nature of small disturbances is in general of the fourth order, but may be reduced to the third by a proper choice of the value of the mean overflow.

Theory of Differential Gearing.

In some contrivances the main shaft is connected with the governor by a wheel or system of wheels which are capable of rotation round an axis, which is itself also capable of rotation about the axis of the main shaft. These two axes may be at right angles, as in the ordinary system of differential bevel wheels; or they may be parallel, as in several contrivances adapted to clockwork.

Let ξ and η represent the angular position about each of these axes respectively, θ that of the main shaft, and ϕ that of the governor; then θ and ϕ are linear functions of ξ and η, and the motion of any point of the system can be expressed in terms either of ξ and η or of θ and ϕ.

Let the velocity of a particle whose mass is m resolved in the direction of x be

$$(50) \qquad \frac{dx}{dt} = p_1 \frac{d\xi}{dt} + q_1 \frac{d\eta}{dt}$$

with similar expressions for the other co-ordinate directions, putting suffixes 2 and 3 to denote the values of p and q for these directions. Then Lagrange's equation of motion becomes

$$(51) \qquad \Xi \delta\xi + H\delta\eta = \Sigma m \left(\frac{d^2x}{dt^2}\delta x + \frac{d^2y}{dt^2}\delta y + \frac{d^2z}{dt^2}\delta z \right) = 0$$

where Ξ and H are the forces tending to increase ξ and η respectively, no force being supposed to be applied at any other point.

Now putting

$$(52) \qquad \delta x = p_1 d\xi + q_1 d\eta$$

and

$$(53) \qquad \frac{d^2x}{dt^2} = p_1 \frac{d^2\xi}{dt^2} + q_1 \frac{d^2\eta}{dt^2}$$

the equation becomes

$$(54) \qquad \left(\Xi - \Sigma mp^2 \frac{d^2\xi}{dt^2} - \Sigma mpq \frac{d^2\eta}{dt^2} \right) \delta\xi + \left(H - \Sigma mpq \frac{d^2\xi}{dt^2} - \Sigma mq^2 \frac{d^2\eta}{dt^2} \right) \delta\eta = 0$$

and since $\delta\xi$ and $\delta\eta$ are independent, the coefficient of each must be zero.

If we now put

$$(55) \qquad \Sigma \left(mp^2 \right) = L, \ \Sigma \left(mpq \right) = M, \ \Sigma \left(mqp^2 \right) = N$$

where $p^2 = p_1^2 + p_2^2 + p_3^2$, $pq = p_1q_1 + p_2q_2 + p_3q_3$, and $q^2 = q_1^2 + q_2^2 + q_3^2$, the equations of motion will be

$$(56) \qquad \Xi = L\frac{d^2\xi}{dt^2} + M\frac{d^2\eta}{dt^2}$$

$$(57) \qquad H = M\frac{d^2\xi}{dt^2} + N\frac{d^2\eta}{dt^2}$$

If the apparatus is so arranged that $M = 0$, then the two motions will be independent of each other; and the motions indicated by ξ and η will be about conjugate axes — that is, about axes such that the rotation round one of them does not tend to produce a force about the other.

Now let Θ be the driving-power of tile shaft on the differential system, and Φ that of the differential system on the governor; then the equation of motion becomes

$$(58) \qquad \Theta\delta\theta + \Phi\delta\phi + \left(\Xi - L\frac{d^2\xi}{dt^2} + M\frac{d^2\eta}{dt^2} \right) \delta\xi + \left(H - M\frac{d^2\xi}{dt^2} + N\frac{d^2\eta}{dt^2} \right) \delta\eta = 0$$

and if

$$(59) \qquad \begin{aligned} \delta\xi &= P\delta\theta + Q\delta\phi \\ \delta\eta &= R\delta\theta + S\delta\phi \end{aligned}$$

and if we put

$$(60) \qquad \begin{aligned} L' &= LP^2 + 2MPR + NR^2 \\ M' &= LPQ + M(PS + QR) + NRS \\ N' &= LQ^2 + 2MQS + NS^2 \end{aligned}$$

the equations of motion in θ and ϕ will be

(61)
$$\Theta + P\Xi + QH = L'\frac{d^2\theta}{dt^2} + M'\frac{d^2\phi}{dt^2}$$
$$\Phi + R\Xi + SH = M'\frac{d^2\theta}{dt^2} + N'\frac{d^2\phi}{dt^2}$$

If $M' = 0$, then the motions in θ and ϕ will be independent of each other. If M is also 0, then we have the relation

(62)
$$LPQ + MRS = 0$$

and if this is fulfilled, the disturbances of the motion in θ will have no effect on the motion in ϕ. The teeth of the differential system in gear with the main shaft and the governor respectively will then correspond to the centres of percussion and rotation of a simple body, and this relation will be mutual.

In such differential systems a constant force, H, sufficient to keep the governor in a proper state of efficiency, is applied to the axis η, and the motion of this axis is made to work a valve or a break on the main shaft of the machine. Ξ in this case is merely the friction about the axis of ξ. If the moments of inertia of the different parts of the system are so arranged that $M' = 0$, then the disturbance produced by a blow or a jerk on the machine will act instantaneously on the valve, but will not communicate any impulse to the governor.

Index

V

Veblen, T.
  economist of bling 7-8
Versailles 64
Vietnam War
  cost of 67

W

Wobbly Bridge 129
Wobbly economy 129-130
Wobbly jet 130-132
World War I
  peace treaty 64-65
World War II 64-65

Z

Zimbabwe
  hyperinflation 21